BBC TEST MATCH SPECIAL TEAM

THE · ASHES

· highlights since 1948 ·

BBC BOOKS

BBC TEST MATCH SPECIAL TEAM

THE · ASHES

· highlights since 1948 ·

BBC BOOKS

SPORTS EDITIONS LIMITED

Managing Director	Richard Dewing
Art Director	Mary Hamlyn
Designers	Sandra Cowell
	Rob Kelland
	Adrian Waddington
Copy Editor	Mark Baldwin
Indexer	Valerie Lewis Chandler

First published in 1989 by BBC Books, a division of
BBC Enterprises Limited

BBC Enterprises Ltd., Woodlands, 80 Wood Lane
London W12 OTT

Copyright © Sports Editions Limited

ISBN 0 563 20778 7

BBC BOOKS

Produced, edited and designed by Sports Editions Limited,
3 Greenlea Park, Prince George's Road, London SW19 2JD.

Set in 11½pt Ehrhardt
Typeset by Tunbridge Wells Typesetting Services Limited
Printed in Great Britain by Mackays of Chatham

Photographic Acknowledgements

ALLSPORT/Adrian Murrell 18 (above), 49 (above), 104 (above), 139, 140, 142-149, 152, 154, 156, 159, 161, 162, 164 (below), 166-174, 175 (below), 176, 179, 180, 182, 183, 185, 186, 188. *The Cricketer* 11 (below), 21 (below), 24, 25, 26, 36, 38, 41 (below), 62, 68, 85 (below), 95, 96, 102 (left), 106 (above), 110, 138. *Patrick Eager* 98, 102 (right), 106 (below), 114 (above), 118, 119, 132 (above), 136, 155, 164 (above). *Hulton Deutsch Collection* 11 (above), 16, 17, 20, 22, 27, 28, 30, 33, 35, 37 (below), 43, 46 (below), 48, 52 (below), 70, 71, 72, 73 (below), 74, 79, 81, 82, 84, 85 (above), 86, 87, 89, 92, 103, 107, 108, 112, 114 (below), 116, 117 (below), 123, 124, 129 (above). *Ken Kelly* 10, 15, 18 (below), 21 (above), 39, 41 (above), 50, 54, 67, 73 (above), 76, 100, 104 (below), 134 (below), 175 (above three). *Press Association* 37 (above), 65, 97, 117 (above), 120, 121, 122, 125, 129 (below), 130, 131, 132 (below), 133, 134 (above), 135. *Sport and General* 12, 34, 40, 44, 45, 46 (above), 49, 60 (above), 61, 64, 66. *Surrey County Cricket Club* 14, 53, 59, 60 (below and centre), 61 (below and right). *Topham Picture Library* 52 (above), 57, 77, 90.

Front Cover Photographs (clockwise from top left) *ALLSPORT/Adrian Murrell, The Cricketer, Hulton Deutsch Collection, ALLSPORT/Adrian Murrell, ALLSPORT/Adrian Murrell, ALLSPORT/Ben Radford, ALLSPORT, Adrian Murrell, Sport and General, The Cricketer, Hulton Deutsch Collection, Hulton Deutsch Collection, ALLSPORT/Adrian Murrell, Hulton Deutsch Collection, The Cricketer.*

CONTENTS

ACKNOWLEDGEMENTS

The work of several broadcasters is represented in this book, some of them no longer alive, but all preserved in the BBC Sound Archives: Rex Alston, Jack Bannister, Jim Burke, Michael Charlton, Dennis Cometti, Graham Dawson, George Duckworth, Jack Fingleton, Charles Fortune, Bill Frindall, Alan Gibson, Arthur Gilligan, Lindsay Hassett, Robert Hudson, Bernard Kerr, Tony Lewis, Alan McGilvray, Alan Marks, Jim Maxwell, Johnny Moyes, Bob Richardson, Paul Sheahan, E. W. Swanton.

Also appearing here, in their capacity as captain of their respective countries are: Sir Donald Bradman, Sir Leonard Hutton and Tony Greig.

For their efforts in translating the words of all these men from tape to paper we are particularly grateful to Louise Jones and Shirley Clark. A number of record books had, obviously, to be consulted in the preparation of this book, top of the list as always being Wisden's Cricketer's Almanack, but three other works deserve special mention: 'Farewell to Cricket' by Don Bradman, 'Len Hutton' by Gerald Howat and 'The Ashes Crown the Year' by Jack Fingleton.

Several sources of archive photographs provided pictures of specific incidents – Bradman bowled Hollies nought etc., and all are acknowledged in the index section of this book. Special thanks are due to Ken Kelly, Richard Wilson and Peter Large, librarian at Surrey County Cricket Club, as well as Adrian Murrell, Patrick Eager, Mavis Streeton, Gina Orr, Abigail Sims and Matt Homes at Allsport. We are also indebted to Richard Dewing and Mary Hamlyn and their trusty team of designers at Sports Editions: Sandra Cowell, Rob Kelland and Adrian Waddington. Invaluable research was undertaken by Hayters Sports Reporting Agency.

Peter Baxter and Peter Hayter

INTRODUCTION

Sixty years ago, in the early days of sports broadcasting, it was believed that cricket was an impossible subject for radio commentary. The pace, insisted such venerated pioneers of the art as H. B. T. Wakelam, was far too slow for the medium. It took Howard Marshall in the thirties to show that the gradual build-up to each peak of violent action as the bowler bowls is actually the perfect recipe for descriptive commentary.

This book is as much a celebration of that art as of some of the dramatic moments that the last forty years have produced in the greatest of all cricket contests – the battles for the Ashes.

Many people remember where they were and what they were doing as they listened to the thrilling climax, for instance, of the Leeds Test in 1981 as Bob Willis bowled out Australia after Ian Botham's devastating innings. Gentlemen abed in England will recall early winter mornings in 1974/75 when the transistor radio under the pillow brought them news of the ravages of Lillee and Thomson being wrought on the other side of the world. Australians over 50 might remember some all-night party during which they heard of the prodigious deeds of Bradman and Morris as Australia chased over 400 runs in a day. And, indeed, that match at Headingley in 1948 is the starting point for this nostalgic trip.

The narrative text is punctuated with transcripts of commentaries on many of the crucial moments and accompanied by interviews containing memories and opinions of members of the Radio 3 'Test Match Special' team – in the case of Trevor Bailey and Fred Trueman, often of matches in which they were playing. Commentary, being the unscripted immediate reaction of the commentator to what he sees happening in front of him, sometimes makes untidy reading. Sentences are frequently unfinished or not strictly grammatical. The passages of commentary have only been adjusted to make them more readable, but otherwise represent exactly what was said at the time on the air.

Our selection of the matches was very much a matter

of personal choice of the games that had stirred our memory. Great players from Bradman to Botham obviously loom large in our story, but there is also the 'what-ever-happened-to?' brigade, such as Bob Massie and David Steele who each seized his chance at Lord's. There are the tales of romantic recalls to the colours for Freddie Brown, Cyril Washbrook and Colin Cowdrey.

I know that our choice will stir many memories, and present glimpses of cricket history in an entertaining way. The Ashes in their historic urn have always been the most fiercely contested of trophies, but often stirring individual performances have transcended the result.

That is part of the charm of cricket.

Peter Baxter
Soulbury
March 1989

AUSTRALIA IN ENGLAND 1948

The Fourth Test, **Headingley,** *July 22-27*
The Fifth Test, **The Oval,** *August 14-18*
Commentators **Rex Alston, John Arlott, Alan McGilvray, E. W. Swanton, Bernard Kerr** *with expert comments by* **A. E. R. Gilligan.**

On Friday April 16, 1948 the S.S. Strathaird docked at Tilbury to discharge on English shores arguably the greatest ever team of cricketers. For their captain, Don Bradman, the Australian tour was to be a final triumphant progress, laughing in the face of his own self doubts before his team had left home. But, as he undertook the start of countless official functions in that opening week of the tour he made it clear that this would mark the end of his cricket career. Most of these functions involved him in making a speech, frequently broadcast live, as was the Cricket Writers' Club Dinner, under the chairmanship of E. W. Swanton, at which the Don demonstrated his flair for public speaking …

Don Bradman

❝Having listened to the eulogistic remarks of your chairman, I feel that we are indeed a very popular band of cricketers. I sincerely hope that he will think the same of us about the middle of September, even though we do not accede to the request that he makes of us to allow the English team to beat us in the intervening period … Now I understand that this gathering this evening is being broadcast. I didn't know about that until I received a letter from a little English boy and he said in this letter, "I'll be listening in to you tonight, that is if the wireless doesn't break down as it usually does." He evidently hasn't got much faith in the wireless. But anyway I hope that that little boy is listening in and that the wireless hasn't broken down because I want to take this opportunity of sending from Australia a message to the people who are listening tonight of goodwill and encouragement from our land. And in particular a message to the children of this country, because we know that they are having a very tough time. We can assure them that Australia is behind them in spirit and that she will continue to do all she possibly can to make their lot a little easier in the future …

We're going to do everything we can to make this a happy and successful tour. We'll do everything we can to beat you … and I do feel sure that when the time comes to lay down our bats at the end of the summer, we shall all regret the passing of a great season and I hope that we will all have done much to restore to its proper pedestal the greatest game in the British Empire.❞ Don Bradman

The Australians arrive at Tilbury

How evocative is that talk of Empire now. But the fact that Bradman was able to convey such sentiments and messages of support, without sounding in the least outrageous, is a measure of the special position he occupied in popular affection. His powerful team was able to contribute in some measure to the raising of post war spirits.

The Australians would not have been able to shine to such an extent without a fair opposition and there was, despite the deprivations of war, talent in England. To be fair, some of it was past its best, some yet to mature. But what would modern selectors not give for an England team which includes names like Hutton, Washbrook, Edrich, Compton, Laker, Bedser and Evans?

Lindwall and Miller were a pair to cause apprehension in any batting side, but it was the fast-medium left arm bowling of Bill Johnston which had the most effect in the First Test at Trent Bridge, capturing 9 wickets in all and ensuring an eight wicket victory for Australia despite injury to Lindwall. Compton's second innings 184 ended, tragically, when he slipped and fell on his stumps trying to avoid a Miller bouncer, in reply to centuries by Bradman and Hassett. At Lord's, Australia's winning margin was 409 runs in a match illuminated by further centuries from Morris and Barnes and eight wickets from Lindwall. By drawing at Old Trafford,

Denis Compton falls on his stumps

Australia secured the Ashes, though they could be said to have been saved by the Manchester weather, after a brave century by Compton – interrupted when he was led from the field, having edged a no-ball bouncer from Lindwall into his forehead – and the bowling of Bedser and Pollard had given England a first innings lead of 142 runs.

So the series was decided before the two teams arrived in Leeds for the Fourth Test. The Yorkshire crowds and Bradman had long had a soft spot for each other and the great man had given them some of his finest performances; 334 in 1930, 304 in 1934 and 103 in 1938. For them he was saving his 29th and last Test hundred and, in honour of his never having failed to pass three figures in a Headingley Test, Yorkshire were to make him an honorary life member of the club.

But England had a Yorkshire captain, Norman Yardley, who won the toss and, on a perfect pitch, chose to bat. He and the selectors had, however, already made the fateful decision to leave the Middlesex slow left arm bowler Jack Young out of their twelve. That was of little concern to Yorkshire folk as they watched their own Len Hutton and Lancashire's Cyril Washbrook open the England innings. Hutton had been dropped for the previous Test, Bradman thought at the time on disciplinary grounds, others because he was struggling against Lindwall and Miller and that this was undermining his side's confidence. Yet the selectors had the sense of occasion to bring him back for Headingley and Hutton repaid them in a commanding opening stand with Washbrook. With the score at 168, Australia took the second new ball ...

Len Hutton

JOHN ARLOTT

Lindwall seizes it, and he's going to bowl with the new ball now from the Grandstand End. He goes through the usual Lindwall bout of physical jerks, the shirt is now comfortably loose and it fills with wind as he comes up now from the Grandstand End ... bowls to Hutton ... a magnificent outswinger ... hit for four.

Now, that was hit on the half volley by Hutton for four and a difficult ball it was to cope with. Over its last two yards

it went eight inches, it moved from the line of the middle-and-off, clean outside the off stump and Hutton, right over it, hit it firmly past the somnolent Toshack at point for four runs. And now here comes Lindwall again to Hutton, and that … is a magnificent inswinger that bowls him, off his pads. Hutton was out for 81, but his replacement was the ebullient Bill Edrich, just the man to help Washbrook to three figures …

JOHN ARLOTT
The noose of the field is tight round him now as he struggles for this hundred. And Toshack is a nasty man to complete your hundred against. Here he is, bowls to Washbrook, off the inside edge. England 189 for 1, Washbrook not out 100, his first hundred against Australia in England, made in three hours forty minutes with 16 fours.

Washbrook continued until the final over of that first day, taking his own score to 143 and the second wicket partnership to exactly 100. The nightwatchman was Alec Bedser, Yardley saving Denis Compton for the next day. Another new ball was available then, on a dark and cloudy morning, but Bedser stayed with Edrich through a difficult first hour until, as the sun came out, he decided it was his duty to hit out or get out. By lunch the third wicket stand had passed 100 and the off-spinner, Ian Johnson had to wait until nearly three o'clock before he separated them after 155 had been added. First he had Bedser caught and bowled for 79, and then …

REX ALSTON
Bowling rather well now, Ian Johnson, not dropping 'em short and, of course, with his tail up, having got that wicket. In to Edrich and that's a baddish ball … but he's got a wicket though. Edrich is out, caught by Morris at midwicket.
At 423 for two, the extent of England's ambition had seemed boundless, but Ian Johnson had opened the trap-door and batsmen proceeded to fall though.

ALAN McGILVRAY
Now, Miller is about to bowl to Yardley. He's bowled, all out, England are all out for 496. That was a bad shot by Yardley, he endeavoured to clip that ball and it came in at him. I mentioned, last over, a ball that Miller bowled to him

ENGLAND
FIRST INNINGS
168-1

ENGLAND
FIRST INNINGS
189-1

ENGLAND
FIRST INNINGS
426-4

ENGLAND
FIRST INNINGS
496 all out

Alec Bedser

AUSTRALIA
FIRST INNINGS
13-1

AUSTRALIA
FIRST INNINGS
68-3

that swung very late – on this occasion Yardley tried to square cut it, but the ball dipped late. Its not as healthy a score as I anticipated after the start this morning; nevertheless it's still a very good one and it's going to be hard for Australia to win from here. But I'm still not prepared to say they can't, even if John Arlott doesn't agree. He says England can't lose. I think that you never know in the game of cricket.

By the end of the second day Australia's task was made to look even steeper by Bedser . . .

 REX ALSTON
And now here's Bedser to Morris and he's out . . . caught. Morris, caught Cranston at mid-wicket – a good catch – off Bedser for six. The ball was hit quite hard and was at the full stretch of Cranston's right hand. He had to move pretty quickly and he held it in both hands. And so, the very dangerous Morris, from an England point of view, is out for six, and Australia, on the long road to make 496, are 13 for one. And in a moment there'll be a burst of applause because it'll be Bradman . . . and here it is.

How splendid to be so certain in advance of that ovation. The next morning Dick Pollard, Bedser's new ball partner in this match, removed Lindsay Hassett for 13 and, two balls later, was bowling to Bradman . . .

 REX ALSTON
Now the field has been changed and Hutton has been put in his pet spot to try to catch Bradman. He's been moved across from the gully where he was for Hassett and Miller, and Cranston has been moved near to square leg from long leg. And now, Pollard to Bradman . . . and he's bowled him.

To have Bradman back in the pavilion for just 33 was riches beyond measure for England. Keith Miller was now joined by the nineteen-year-old Neil Harvey, playing in only his third Test and his first against England. Although his last Test innings had been 153 against India in Melbourne, his display of confidence as he joined his senior partner was perhaps a little precocious. Miller recalls Harvey's words of greeting: "Hey, Nugget, what's going on out here? Let's get stuck into them." Miller did farm the bowling to the extent of trying to spare Harvey the wiles of Laker, who was turning the ball away from the left hander, but the pair brought Australia right back into the game with a glorious partnership of 121 which only ended when Miller lunged at Yardley and was caught. 189 for 3. Loxton joined Harvey, who was making a memorable Ashes debut . . .

REX ALSTON
The total – 272 for 4. The field changes over and now there are three more balls this over. Laker to Harvey, Harvey having a look round at the field. Harvey 99 and here's this ball . . . he drives him, they're trying for the single and he's got it.

Laker eventually had his revenge, bowling Harvey for 112 but Loxton, in tremendous form, hit five sixes and nine fours in an innings of 93. However, when Yardley had bowled him and Laker had accounted for Johnson and Saggers, Australia were still 141 in arrears at 355 for 8. Coming in at number eight, Ray Lindwall now found great support from Johnston and Toshack as he made 77 and the Australian tail wagged its way to 458, only 38 behind.

For the second time in the match Hutton and Washbrook passed 100 for the first wicket. They both went at 129, but Compton and Edrich made 103 for the third wicket at better than a run a minute. After their departure Lindwall and Johnston effected a minor mid-innings collapse, halted by Godfrey Evans. At the close of the fourth day England were 362 for 8 – exactly 400 ahead.

There were many who felt that England had already delayed the declaration unnecessarily. Certainly the team felt that the match was at least safe and possibly won.

But Norman Yardley continued for two overs on the final morning to give himself the choice of the heaviest roller in order to break up the pitch still further.

Australia's target was 404 to win in a day less fifteen minutes. It was a task that had never been accomplished in the fourth innings of a Test. Furthermore, the pitch was taking spin and the ball was lifting and turning sharply, and most of the Australian side had no thought of victory.

Bradman admits to having been undecided, especially when Hassett was caught and bowled by Compton for 17 at 57 for 1. But Yardley was now feeling the

Neil Harvey

ENGLAND
SECOND INNINGS
362-8

absence of that second specialist spinner. By mid-morning, he had already had to bring on Compton to support Laker, whose length was erratic, and now he turned to the even more occasional spin of Hutton. In the half-hour before lunch Bradman helped Arthur Morris add another 64 runs and his mind was made up: They were going for them. Certainly, luck was turning their way. Just after lunch Compton had Bradman dropped at slip by Crapp and there were more chances to come.

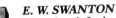

E. W. SWANTON
Now here's Laker bowling again to Bradman, Bradman on 99 and he pushes that one very carefully to short leg. He's made 99. Here's Laker bowling to him, it's a short one and that's his hundred.

The normally impeccable Evans was well below par. He should have stumped Morris at 32 and frustration mounted.

E. W. SWANTON
Here's Denis Compton bowling now to Morris and he's caught, a catch, . . . no a miss, a miss at short leg . . . dropped by Laker. Morris hooked a short one and Laker seemed to have it in his hands. And this time, a short one which Morris hooks round the corner for four. Well, we've seen two very difficult chances in the last few balls and England haven't been able to take either of them.

In modern Test cricket no fielding side would deliver as many as the 109 overs that England sent down that day especially as that Bradman/Morris stand grew more threatening. At the time, too, it was felt that the left-hand/right-hand combination of the pair was actually slowing the over-rate. Eventually Yardley broke them up, getting Morris for 182, but, by that time, that partnership of 301 had all but done the job. Miller went cheaply and so the young Harvey came in to join his captain . . .

JOHN ARLOTT
There was no leg-spinner in the England side except Hutton or Compton when he bowled his left arm googlies and neither of those looked good enough to worry great batsmen who were bent on taking up England's challenge of fast runs. Well, now, Cranston comes in to bowl to Harvey,

Don Bradman

**AUSTRALIA
SECOND INNINGS
404-3**

Harvey picks him off his toes, hits him to the long-on boundary and he's stolen a stump and the ball has crossed the boundary and it's all over. And we greet our general overseas listeners at the moment when the great crowd surges all across the ground . . . despite the policemen . . . and Australia have won the fourth Test at Headingley by seven wickets.

Two and a half weeks after his romantic triumph at Leeds, Bradman came to the Oval and England came to grief on a pitch underprepared as a result of bad weather – all out for 52 of which Hutton contributed a remarkable 30. But that was just a curtain raiser for the fall of the first Australian wicket. They were already 65 in the lead when Don Bradman took the Test stage for the last time with a bat in his hand and 6,996 Test runs behind him . . .

REX ALSTON
The Australians have been batting now for what, two hours? Just over two hours and a quarter. And here's the applause for Bradman as he comes in. Well, its a wonderful reception, the whole crowd is standing and the England team are joining in and . . . led by Yardley . . . three cheers for the

Don as he gets to the wicket . . . And now the crowd settle down again. Forty minutes left for play and Bradman is now taking guard, Hollies is going to bowl at him and John Arlott shall describe the first ball.

Three cheers for the Don

JOHN ARLOTT
Well I don't think I'm as deadly as you are, Rex. I don't expect to get a wicket, but it's rather good to be here when Don Bradman comes in to bat in his last Test.

And now here's Hollies to bowl to him from the Vauxhall End. He bowls . . . and Bradman goes back across his wicket and pushes the ball gently in the direction of the Houses of Parliament, which are out beyond mid-off. It doesn't go that far, it merely goes to Watkins at silly mid-off, no run, still 117 for one – two slips, a silly mid-off and a forward short leg close to him as Hollies pitches the ball up slowly and . . . he's bowled

Of the countless tributes to Bradman's unique genius, none is more poignant than this extract from the 1949 edition of Wisden, written by R.C. Robertson-Glasgow:

"Don Bradman will bat no more against England, and two contrary feelings dispute within us: relief, that our bowlers will no longer be oppressed by this phenomenon; regret, that a miracle has been removed from among us."

. . . Bradman bowled Hollies nought . . . bowled Hollies nought . . . and what do you say under those circumstances? How . . . I wonder if you see the ball very clearly in your last Test in England, on a ground where you've played some of the biggest cricket of your life and where the opposing side has just stood around you and given you three cheers, and the crowd has clapped you all the way to the wicket. I wonder if you really see the ball at all. Anyway, Bradman went forward, it was Hollies' googly, it clean bowled him, groping right down the pitch and he was just beaten all the way. I think he was completely out of his crease and would have been stumped if it hadn't hit the wicket. He didn't seem to make any attempt to get back, he knew it had bowled him and Australia are 117 for 2 in reply to England's 52.

Later Bradman was to make it clear that he hade no idea at the time that just four runs would have given him a Test average of 100. With a twinkle he suggested that the knowledge might have been all the spur he needed.

His last Test ended in a comfortable innings victory and the 1948 Australians ended their tour unbeaten with a four-nil win in the Test series, and the Ashes safe for at least another eighteen months.

Eric Hollies

Fifth Test, The Oval, 14-18 August 1948
Australia won by an innings and 149 runs

ENGLAND

L. Hutton c Tallon b Lindwall	30	c Tallon b Miller	64
J. G. Dewes b Miller	1	b Lindwall	10
W. J. Edrich c Hassett b Johnston	3	b Lindwall	28
D. Compton c Morris b Lindwall	4	c Lindwall b Johnston	39
J. F. Crapp c Tallon b Miller	0	b Miller	9
*N. W. D. Yardley b Lindwall	7	c Miller b Johnston	9
A. J. Watkins lbw b Johnston	0	c Hassett b Ring	2
†T. G. Evans b Lindwall	1	b Lindwall	8
A. V. Bedser b Lindwall	0	b Johnston	0
J. A. Young b Lindwall	0	not out	3
W. E. Hollies not out	0	c Morris b Johnston	0
Extras (b6)	6	(b9, lb4, nb3)	16
Total	**52**		**188**

AUSTRALIA

S. G. Barnes c Evans b Hollies	61
A. R. Morris run out	196
*D. G. Bradman b Hollies	0
A. L. Hassett lbw b Young	37
K. R. Miller st Evans b Hollies	5
R. N. Harvey c Young b Hollies	17
S. J. E. Loxton c Evans b Edrich	15
R. R. Lindwall c Edrich b Young	9
†D. Tallon c Crapp b Hollies	31
D. T. Ring c Crapp b Bedser	9
W. A. Johnston not out	0
Extras (b4, lb2, nb3)	9
Total	**389**

BOWLING

AUSTRALIA	O	M	R	W		O	M	R	W
Lindwall	16.1	5	20	6	–	25	3	50	3
Miller	8	5	5	2	–	15	6	22	2
Johnston	16	4	20	2	–	27.3	12	40	4
Loxton	2	1	1	0	–	10	2	16	0
Ring					–	28	13	44	1

ENGLAND	O	M	R	W	
Bedser	31.2	9	61	1	–
Watkins	4	1	19	0	–
Young	51	16	118	2	–
Hollies	56	14	131	5	–
Compton	2	0	6	0	–
Edrich	9	1	38	1	–
Yardley	5	1	7	0	–

ENGLAND fall of wickets
FIRST INNINGS: 1-2, 2-10, 3-17, 4-23, 5-35, 6-42, 7-45, 8-45, 9-47.
SECOND INNINGS: 1-20, 2-64, 3-125, 4-153, 5-164, 6-167, 7-178, 8-181, 9-188.
AUSTRALIA fall of wickets
FIRST INNINGS: 1-117, 2-117, 3-226, 4-243, 5-265, 6-304, 7-332, 8-359, 9-389.

First Test at Trent Bridge, June 10-15
Australia won by eight wickets
England 165 (Laker 63, Johnston 5-36)
and 441 (Compton 184, Hutton 74, Evans
50); Australia 509 (Bradman 138, Hassett
137, Barnes 62) and 98-2 (Barnes 64*).

Second Test at Lord's, June 24-29
Australia won by 409 runs
Australia 350 (Morris 105, Tallon 53) and
460-7 dec (Barnes 141, Bradman 89,
Miller 74, Morris 62); England 215
(Compton 53, Lindwall 5-70) and 186
(Toshack 5-40)

Third Test at Old Trafford, July 8-13
Match drawn
England 363 (Compton 145*) and 174-3
dec (Washbrook 85*, Edrich 53); Australia
221 (Morris 51) and 92-1 (Morris 54*).

Fourth Test at Headingley, July 22-27
Australia won by 7 wickets
England 496 (Washbrook 143, Edrich 111,
Hutton 81, Bedser 79) and 365-8 dec
(Compton 66, Washbrook 65, Hutton 57,
Edrich 54); Australia 458 (Harvey 112,
Loxton 93, Lindwall 77, Miller 58) and
404-3 (Morris 182, Bradman 173*).

A U S T R A L I A   I N   E N G L A N D   1 9 5 3

The Second Test, **Lords,** *June 25-30, 1953*
The Fifth Test, **The Oval,** *August 15-19*
Commentators **Rex Alston, John Arlott and Bernard Kerr,**
with summaries by **E. W. Swanton.**

66The amazing thing about 1953 was that no game ever seemed to run the same way for two successive days; often not for two successive sessions. And this was, I think, the most exciting drawn match I've ever seen.99
                                  John Arlott

1953 was a royal year. The new Elizabethan age had begun and with the young Queen's Coronation came a spirit of hope. It was a year of British achievement; Everest was conquered, British aircraft were blazing new trails in the skies and, in the field of human endeavour, British runners were nudging the elusive four-minute-mile barrier. In cricket, Bradman and the war years had combined to keep the Ashes away from England for nearly nineteen years.

Jack Fingleton was to entitle his account of that series, 'The Ashes Crown the Year'. But it was so nearly a different story. In the first Test at Trent Bridge, begun a week after the Coronation, Australia had taken a first innings lead, but Alec Bedser had heroically bowled England into a potentially winning position with 14 wickets before the weather took a hand to thwart them. Australia's popular captain, Lindsay Hassett, scored a century there and he and his side, which still contained several of the 1948 stars, were to demand more England heroics at Lord's in the Second Test.

The first surprise emerged before that match when the chairman of selectors, Freddie Brown, was named in the England team. The captain, Len Hutton, had insisted on his inclusion, probably remembering his great-hearted efforts in Australia a couple of years before. It was not perhaps quite the shock such a move might have been in recent years as Brown was still playing county cricket for Northamptonshire.

As he was to do throughout the series, Hassett won the toss on June 25 in glorious weather with the 'ground full' notices posted at all the gates. Hassett chose to bat and, with Morris, put up 65 for the first wicket. The wicket of Morris for 30 was England's only success of the morning, almost inevitably another scalp for Bedser.

Harvey became Bedser's second victim soon after the interval, lbw for 59, an innings which had taken him past his thousand runs for the tour. Hassett and Harvey had added 125 for the second wicket, but at least when Hassett reached his hundred, he gave the bowlers some respite by retiring with muscular trouble. Wardle, with fresh batting on which to practice his wiles soon had Hole and Benaud cheaply and then lured Miller, in attacking mood, into trying to hit him out of the ground a second time, to be bowled for 25 and it was 240 for 5.

The next day started with another success for Johnny Wardle, who was proving a more than adequate replacement for the injured Tony Lock. Bowling round the wicket, he had Ring lbw for 18. That, however, only brought back Lindsay Hassett, a hundred already to his name, though still troubled by his arm, to join the always threatening Davidson. Hassett held an affectionate place in British hearts.

Hutton and Hassett toss up

It was Wardle who needed the sense of humour at this stage, as he had Hassett twice dropped in the slips. At last, Bailey held on to one in the gully off Bedser's bowling and Australia were 291 for 7. It was not the end, though, as Alan Davidson swung the bat to take his own score to 76 in his second Test match and Australia to 346 all out a quarter of an hour after lunch on the second day.

Now Hutton and Kenyon came out to face one of the truly great pairs of opening bowlers …

❝Lindsay was a first class captain. He was also a first class batsman. He also had a most terrific sense of humour; he used to bat almost like a joke. He used, for instance, to exaggerate a defensive stroke. But, as his batting in 1953 shows, when he had taken over as captain, he played with immense responsibility — plus a sense of humour. **❞**   **John Arlott**

Her Majesty the Queen meets the tourists

❝Lindwall (*right*) and Miller used to have a peculiar effect, both in 1948 and in 1953. When those two came on to bowl, they bowled almost in silence. They used to set a chill on English grounds and English supporters lived in dread of them. The trouble was that after the Second World War, as after the First, we were short of fast bowlers and the Australians weren't and that was the real crux of the matter. Certainly Miller and Lindwall had this knack of creating great drama when they bowled.

Ray Lindwall was a master of technique; although his arm was low, he was highly skilful. Keith, of course, could always rise to the occasion and produce the great ball and he could also produce the bouncer — they both could. They were as deadly a fast bowling combination as I ever saw in my life — and I do mean a combination.❞ **John Arlott**

Len Hutton had not enjoyed a true captain's match with three missed catches behind him. He was to make up for those lapses in his own way. His opening partner, Don Kenyon, was caught at leg slip off Lindwall for 3 when the score was 9. Hutton was joined by Tom Graveney and they dominated the day, by the end of which England were 177 for 1. The second wicket, though, fell at that same score to the fourth ball of the third day when Lindwall clean bowled Graveney for 78. That brought in Denis Compton who helped Hutton to a majestic century. He was finally out just before lunch, caught at backward square leg off Bill Johnston for 145.

At 279 for 3, England were in a healthy position, especially with runs coming at such an encouraging pace. But the afternoon brought a collapse, with the next six wickets going down for fifty including Compton, caught at slip off Richie Benaud for 57. Wardle and Statham took England into the lead before Davidson ended it at 372 – 26 runs ahead. Lindwall, had taken 5 for 66.

When England dismissed Hassett with only 3 on the board, caught behind off Statham, Miller came in ahead of Harvey, in determined mood, and ensured that Australia were well into the lead for no further loss by the close. On the Monday morning Morris and Miller increased that healthy position in lively fashion before

Morris miscued a ball from Compton and was caught at square leg for 89. Miller was now joined by Neil Harvey with Australia 142 ahead and the game at their mercy. After lunch, and after Miller had got to his hundred, England applied a brake as Bedser and Wardle dismissed both of them. When Benaud joined Graeme Hole at 235 for 4 the game was nicely in the balance …

JOHN ARLOTT
248 for four, Australia … twelve to Hole, five to Benaud. Even the score's not important, the fact is that the winning or losing of this match can be in the balance now. Wardle to Hole, pitched up outside the off-stump, Hole flogs that off the back foot, Bailey fields very well a bumping ball at cover. And now before Bedser starts another over from the Nursery End, let's pass the commentary over to Bernard Kerr.

BERNARD KERR
Four wickets down for 248. Benaud is facing Bedser who is bowling magnificently, putting everything he's got into it and, Benaud lifts it and he's out, caught at mid-on by Graveney. Benaud's out, caught Graveney, bowled Bedser and now Australia are 248 for five, Benaud scoring five.

A crucial blow struck for England with the lead still in manageable proportions, but Davidson again looked ominously aggressive. Brown, however, caught him in two minds for a straightforward caught and bowled. Eleven more runs came before Brown took the wicket of Hole, and Lindsay Ring soon became his third victim. At 308 for 8 Australia were 282 ahead.

Ray Lindwall then scored 50 in as many minutes before Brown and Bedser were able to finish the innings off. Brown's leg breaks had made him the most successful of the bowlers with 4 for 82 but the effect of Lindwall's hitting had been to set England 343 to win on the last day plus the remaining hour.

By the end of the fifth over Lindwall had sent back both openers with only 10 runs on the board. Soon afterwards Bill Johnston had Graveney caught behind and England were 12 for 3. Compton and Watson survived to the close at 20 for 3, but most believed that only disaster awaited.

**AUSTRALIA
SECOND INNINGS
248-5**

❝It did rather look as if England had no chance of saving the match on the final day. Willie Watson, *(right)* had been dropped that night and so it could have been about 16 for 4 and I don't think anybody expected them to hold out against bowling like that — Miller, Lindwall, Johnston, Davidson and the leg spinners — it was a pretty good attack.❞

John Arlott

❝The last day started, as far as I was concerned, travelling up from Southend to Fenchurch Street with my wife and reading the papers. They'd all written us off and I felt a little bit narked by this because, personally, although I wasn't going to say we were going to save the game, I hadn't even gone in to bat. It did seem rather harsh to be written off before one had even gone to the wicket.

The mood in the dressing room was not quite so optimistic. Willie, of course, was a quiet, peace-loving individual and he was prepared to go out and bat for his life which was exactly what he did. We lost Compton, who really was the person on whom everyone reckoned our chances rested, and quite rightly, because he was easily the best player. He departed round about 12.15, when I went out and joined Willie. I think the nicest story — it may be apocryphal — is of the Scottish Rugby international who decided to come along to the last day simply because they served very good draught beer at Lord's all day. He bought his first pint just before lunch and didn't realise it had been knocked over until the tea interval. I think that sort of sums it all up. It was a very tense day.❞

Trevor Bailey, *(right)*

With the clock always against them, the ball turning from the hands of the Australian spinners, Ring, Benaud and Johnson and the score 73 for 4 when they came together Trevor Bailey and Willie Watson, the last pair of front-line batsmen, relied on staunch defence. Frustration set in amongst the Australians as Hassett rang the changes in his attack to try for that vital breakthrough …

Throughout the long afternoon the recalled Freddie Brown waited, padded up, on the dressing room balcony. He came inside at lunch at 116 for 4 to witness Bailey

24

taking Watson's lunch as well as his own, and again at tea at 183 for 4 by which time Watson was 84 and Bailey 39. Even then the match was far from safe for England if the pair were to be separated. But on they went. Fifty minutes after the interval came Bailey's half century – three and three-quarter hours of concentration. His finest hour?

Ten minutes after Bailey's fifty came Watson's century and still the Australians could not break the partnership. The end, when it did come was something of a surprise, as Watson got a fine edge to first slip off Ring and after 5 hours and 45 minutes of patience and application his innings was over. As so often happens with big partnerships Bailey followed almost immediately, caught at point off Ring. In four and a quarter hours they had put on 161 together for the fifth wicket. They had almost made it safe, but Australia still had half an hour to try to capture the last four wickets.

Coming in now, Freddie Brown was not to be dictated to by the spinners, even with the fielders clustered round his bat. He played his shots in scoring 28 in twenty minutes he was at the wicket and claims that it was his first defensive shot that got him out, caught at slip off Benaud. But by that time the match really was safe.

66 Technically, no. It was an exciting moment but it certainly wasn't the best innings I played, but I suppose in terms of the situation it just happened to be right at that particular time. It was the situation that made it.

My attitude was that I expected every ball to do the unexpected, to do something. So I was looking for the ball that was going to pitch on leg stump and hit off stump or pitch off and hit leg. It was a matter of sheer concentration on making absolutely sure you played the good ball. In fact, the most dangerous ball is the really bad ball because that is when you lose concentration.

It got very tense. In fact I found I was more worried after I was out, when I was back in the dressing room and I could do absolutely nothing about it than when I was actually batting, because I didn't think about anything else except batting when I was out there.

Willie was a little unlucky. I think he thinks to this day that he was not strictly speaking out. I played a ghastly shot and had only myself to blame. But as far as I was concerned it was worse when I was back in the pavilion thinking "you fool", why did you get out then?" because I shouldn't have done. 99

Trevor Bailey

66In the end we got quite close to the eventual target but we never considered it and of course, to be perfectly honest if they had wanted to shut the game up they could have done and we would never have got near it. But they pressed on. They thought they were going to win. I think we, by and large, thought they were going to win and we simply held on as long as we could. It was very exciting. The whole thing was enormous fun.

It was a glorious Test match. People say draws are bad for cricket. Some draws are bad for cricket, but exciting draws — and this was a very exciting draw — are very good for cricket.

The most intriguing thing about the stand is that it seems to get longer and longer as time goes by. It was quite a long stand but it wasn't all that long. There were quite a lot of people who did see it, but not the quarter of a million who have told me they saw it.**99**

Trevor Bailey

The Manchester rain had the last word in the Third Test, although Wardle took 4 for 7 in 5 overs to finish the match with Australia in some disarray at 35 for 8 in their second innings. In the Fourth Test at Headingley,

Australia had very much the better of the draw. So at the Oval, the only resolved match of the series, the narrow advantage of a 31 run first innings lead for England was greatly enhanced by Laker and Lock in the second innings. Lock took 5 for 45 and Laker 4 for 75 to leave England needing only 132 runs for the Ashes.

❝The drama of it all. The day we'd all been waiting for because it looked as if we were going to win and the excitement built up all day. The great moment came when the Middlesex twins were together and it was obvious they were going to win. In the penultimate over Hassett put himself on to bowl, and for the the last over — I think there was something like 5 needed — Morris was put on. He bowled a half volley to Edrich which he hit up to mid-off which gave Compton the strike. Compers swept one round towards the boundary and the whole crowd ran on. But Davidson stuck out a claw and stopped it so they all had to go back again.

Then, the next ball was outside the leg stump … and we'll never know whether it reached the boundary because the crowd swarmed on and swallowed it.

The interesting thing about that final ball was that it made Morris the most televised bowler of the age. That shot of the final sweep was used in all the television shops to show off the brand new sets. If you walked along your High Street you couldn't see for hundreds of Arthur Morrises bowling to hundreds of Denis Comptons. The final scenes were marvellous. I was, luckily, on air at the time working for television and I remember shouting: "IT'S THE ASHES! IT'S THE ASHES!" Everyone was hoarse with excitement.❞ **Brian Johnston**

BERNARD KERR

Now Morris, left arm over the wicket to Edrich, another good ball, but Edrich follows that around ... they're going through for a sharp single. Davidson picks the ball up and whizzes it back at the bowler's end but they ran through for the single which makes Edrich now 55, two wickets down for 128 ... four runs short ... Compton facing Morris, Compton on 18, four runs short of the Ashes. Morris to Compton, short and Compton hooks ... Davidson fields and it would have been the Ashes, it would have been four, Davidson fields at fine leg half way to the fence picking it up brilliantly in his left hand.

Morris with his face wreathed in smiles, sends up one to Compton short outside the leg stump, Compton hooks and there's the Ashes! England has won as the ball crashes to the boundary. Two wickets down for 132, with Compton not out 22 and Edrich not out 55. Congratulations, England, on regaining the Ashes and now the crowd are absolutely swarming the ground, they're coming across like ants, thousands and thousands of people right in the centre, keeping away from the actual wicket area. The players are having a most difficult time ... I can see Denis Compton and Bill Edrich being embraced, being kissed by girls and women. I think they'll be bruised by the time they get in. People are now assembled in front of the broadcasting box as this thick crowd forms a lane for the players to make their way to the pavilion.

Crowds in front of the pavilion at
The Oval

This is staggering, highly exciting. As a matter of fact, it's rather moving. From the broadcasting box, you can't see any grass at all, there's just a whole carpet of humanity. Now they're just standing still, I'm afraid they can't move at all — shoulder to shoulder, just as thick as can be. It really is just a wonderful sight.

"We want Len," chanted the crowd as onto the balcony stepped the two captains, Len Hutton and Lindsay Hassett ...

VOICE IN CROWD *"Come on Leonard."*

LEN HUTTON *"Ladies and gentleman, it is very difficult to know what to talk about on these occasions. But I must say how happy and thrilled I feel about it all today. And, of course, for it to happen here at the Oval, which has always been a happy hunting ground for me, is marvellous. But I feel a little bit sorry for my friend Lindsay Hassett, who has had a very hard time this season and what a wonderful opposition captain he has been to play against."*

CROWD *"Hear! Hear"! Applause, Cheers.*

LEN HUTTON *May Australia continue to produce cricketers of the calibre of Lindsay Hassett. He has done so much for the game not only here but in Australia and various parts of the world. I would just like to say thank you all for this wonderful reception. Thank you." Applause.*

ANNOUNCER'S VOICE: *"Ladies and gentlemen, the happy warrior, Lindsay Hassett."*

LINDSAY HASSETT *"I would just like to offer my congratulations to Len and all of the English team. There's no doubt about this victory, they earned it right through from the very first ball right through to the ... second last over anyway. ...*

But it has been wonderful fun and in congratulating Len, I would also like to congratulate all of the players on the wonderful manner in which they've played all of the Test matches this season. As far as I know there hasn't been one incident out of place and I'm quite sure that if you could see how friendly all of the members of the Australian team are with all of the members of the England team, you could hardly understand how they look so hostile towards each other out on the field. I would also like to congratulate the crowd here at the Oval for a very sporting demonstration. I feel rather proud of

29

how the Australian team has played … and it seems obvious to me that you also enjoyed how they played.

We'll be waiting for you in Australia in a couple of years time and I hope, whoever wins out there, that the cricket will be just as enjoyable and the result just as close as this series. Thank you very much."

The obvious affection for Lindsay Hassett and his team served to underline the remark of Sir Robert Menzies that he had never known better ambassadors for Australia.

❝And then there were the celebrations in the pavilion. Later, Jim Laker and Peter May went off with some of the boys to see South Pacific in the West End. When they finally emerged after the show and a spot of refreshment hours later, Laker suddenly remembered he'd promised to meet Lil outside the back door at the Oval at 6.30 … She had not waited.

It was a great moment after nineteen years. It was one of the highlights, of my life, anyhow, to be on the air at that particular time shouting: It's the Ashes … it's the Ashes. Wonderful.**❞**

<u>Brian Johnston</u>

Second Test, Lord's, 25-30 June 1953
Match Drawn

AUSTRALIA

*A. L. Hassett	c Bailey b Bedser	104	c Evans b Statham		3
A. R. Morris	st Evans b Bedser	30	c Statham b Compton		89
R. N. Harvey	lbw b Bedser	59	b Bedser		21
K. R. Miller	b Wardle	25	b Wardle		109
G. B. Hole	c Compton b Wardle	13	lbw b Brown		47
R. Benaud	lbw b Wardle	0	c Graveney b Bedser		5
A. K. Davidson	c Statham b Bedser	76	c and b Brown		15
D. T. Ring	lbw b Wardle	18	lbw b Brown		7
R. R. Lindwall	b Statham	9	b Bedser		50
†G. R. A. Langley	c Watson b Bedser	1	b Brown		9
W. A. Johnston	not out	3	not out		0
Extras	(b4, lb4)	8	(b8, lb5)		13
Total		**346**			**368**

ENGLAND

*L. Hutton	c Hole b Johnston	145	c Hole b Lindwall		5
D. Kenyon	c Davidson b Lindwall	3	c Hassett b Lindwall		2
T. W. Graveney	b Lindwall	78	c Langley b Johnston		2
D. C. S. Compton	c Hole b Benaud	57	lbw b Johnston		33
W. Watson	st Langley b Johnston	4	c Hole b Ring		109
T. E. Bailey	c and b Miller	2	c Benaud b Ring		71
F. R. Brown	c Langley b Lindwall	22	c Hole b Benaud		28
†T. G. Evans	b Lindwall	0	not out		11
J. H. Wardle	b Davidson	23	not out		0
A. V. Bedser	b Lindwall	1			
J. B. Statham	not out	17			
Extras	(b11, lb1, w1, nb7)	20	(b7, lb6, w2, nb6)		21
Total		**372**			**282**

BOWLING

ENGLAND	O	M	R	W		O	M	R	W
Bedser	42.4	8	105	5	–	31.5	8	77	3
Statham	28	7	48	1	–	15	3	40	1
Brown	25	7	53	0	–	27	4	82	4
Bailey	16	2	55	0	–	10	4	24	0
Wardle	29	8	77	4	–	46	18	111	1
Compton					–	3	0	21	1
AUSTRALIA									
Lindwall	23	4	66	5	–	19	3	26	2
Miller	25	6	57	1	–	17	8	17	0
Johnston	35	11	91	2	–	29	10	70	2
Ring	14	2	43	0	–	29	5	84	2
Benaud	19	4	70	1	–	17	6	51	1
Davidson	10.5	2	25	1	–	14	5	13	0
Hole					–	1	1	0	0

AUSTRALIA fall of wickets
FIRST INNINGS: 1-65, 2-190, 3-225, 4-229, 5-240, 6-280, 7-291, 8-330, 9-331.
SECOND INNINGS: 1-3, 2-168, 3-227, 4-235, 5-248, 6-296, 7-305, 8-308, 9-362.
ENGLAND fall of wickets
FIRST INNINGS: 1-9, 2-177, 3-279, 4-291, 5-301, 6-328, 7-328, 8-332, 9-341.
SECOND INNINGS: 1-6, 2-10, 3-12, 4-73, 5-236, 6-246, 7-282.

First Test at Trent Bridge, June 11-16
Match drawn
Australia 249 (Hassett 115, Morris 67, Miller 55, Bedser 7-55) and 123 (Morris 60, Bedser 7-44); England 144 (Lindwall 5-57) and 120-1 (Hutton 60*).

Third Test at Old Trafford, July 9-14
Match drawn
Australia 318 (Harvey 122, Hole 66, Bedser 5-115) and 35-8; England 276 (Hutton 66).

Fourth Test at Headingley, July 23-28
Match drawn
England 167 (Graveney 55, Lindwall 5-54) and 275 (Edrich 64, Compton 61); Australia 266 (Harvey 71, Hole 53, Bedser 6-95) and 147-4.

Fifth Test at The Oval, August 15-19
England won by 8 wickets
Australia 275 (Lindwall 62, Hassett 53) and 162 (Lock 5-45); England 306 (Hutton 82, Bailey 64) and 132-2 (Edrich 55*).

ENGLAND IN AUSTRALIA 1954-55

Commentators **Bernard Kerr, Bob Richardson, Michael Charlton,
Charles Fortune and Alan McGilvray**
Principal Summarisers **Arthur Gilligan, Johnny Moyes**

In August 1954 Pakistan beat England at the Oval. It was their first Test victory and it was not, anyway, the best preparation for the defence of the Ashes won in 1953. Part of England's experimenting at The Oval, though, had been in the fast bowling department, which probably made all the difference. Bailey and Bedser had made way for two debutants, Peter Loader and Frank Tyson. Len Hutton was convinced that fast bowling was the key to success in Australia. Statham was there at The Oval and, like the previous four mentioned, he was on the ship for Australia the next month, but the selectors could not find a place for Fred Trueman. The early matches raised more problems than they solved. Other than Hutton, the batsmen had a wretched time, as did the spinners and, to cap it all, Godfrey Evans was not fully fit.

The England team for Brisbane, therefore, was based on fast bowling, with no specialist spinner. Keith Andrew came in for his first Test behind the stumps and the young Colin Cowdrey, not yet 22, made his debut. Hutton won the toss and became the first England captain to put Australia in to bat in their own country. It was not to be a joyful experience for Bedser, Statham, Tyson and Bailey, all of whom suffered as Australia amassed 601 for 8 declared. Morris and Harvey scored 153 and 162 respectively.

The first three overs of the England innings proved calamitous. Lindwall and Miller sent back Hutton, Simpson and May for 11. Furthermore Compton was absent having broken a bone in his hand while fielding. Cowdrey graced his debut with an innings of 40 and shared a fifth wicket stand of 82 with Trevor Bailey, who made a stylish 88. But after being bowled out for 190, England were following on 411 behind and only praying for a tropical downpour. It did not come. Though this time

May made an encouraging 44 and Edrich 88, England were bowled out for 257 and defeated by an innings and 154 runs.

In the match against Victoria before the Second Test, Peter May made a century, but, perhaps more significantly Frank Tyson took six wickets, five clean bowled. The MCC party cannot have been too disappointed, either, by the news that both Keith Miller and the Australian captain, Ian Johnson, would be unavailable with injuries. Arthur Morris took on the captaincy.

Alec Bedser had been suffering from an attack of shingles and Compton was not yet recovered, so Bob Appleyard and Tom Graveney came into the England side, while, to make room for the spinner he had missed at Brisbane, Hutton dropped Reg Simpson and, as he had with success in the West Indies, decided to open with Bailey. Those two were quickly in action on a grey Sydney morning, as Morris won the toss and put England in. The four-pronged seam attack soon made life uncomfortable and England were all out for a meagre 154. 43 of those runs were due to an adventurous last wicket stand by Wardle and Statham. A shower limited the extent of Australia's batting time that evening, but Bailey captured the valuable wicket of Morris with the last ball of the day.

66 We started with a disaster because we made the mistake — which is now considered a very good thing — of going into the match with four fast bowlers. I thought this absolutely mad at the time and we paid the penalty because we lost very heavily. We went in with Bedser, Statham, Tyson and myself. Compton could bowl a little, and the other spin bowler they were considering was Bill Edrich, who, I think, up to that point, had bowled about three overs in Tests, to bowl off-breaks.

So it was, to my mind, a completely unbalanced attack and we paid the penalty. Today we would say it was a beautiful attack. 99 **Trevor Bailey**

Cowdrey, Hutton and Bedser on voyage

Grey skies persisted on the second day, when Bailey added the wickets of the other opener, Les Favell, for 26 and Jim Burke for 44. Statham and Tyson, too, enjoyed the conditions, though the England attack did feel the absence of Bedser. After being 100 for 2, the Australians lost their sixth wicket when they were still 13 runs behind, but Ron Archer led the way to a substantial enough lead with the top score of 49. At 228 all out the eventual lead was 74, comfortable but by no means as large as the Australians must at one time have been hoping for. Bailey and Tyson had four wickets apiece.

The Monday morning after the rest day was disappointing for England, who wanted a solid start to wipe out the deficit. By the time they had done that, they had lost three wickets to Johnston and Archer. So May and Cowdrey set about giving English cricket followers hope, for this match and for the future. Together they added 116 for the fourth wicket, before Cowdrey lofted a ball from Benaud to be caught for 54. Peter May was on the verge of his first hundred against Australia at 98 not out. England were 204 for 4 at the close of the third day.

❝May was a high quality player, not a genius but a very fine player. Correct and sound, he didn't hook but played well off the back foot. He had no specific weakness, the type of batsman that you wanted to get out. Certainly one of the great post-war international batsmen. Dilip Vengsarkar is probably the nearest modern equivalent in terms of style.

May's greatness was that he could score runs off the good ball with safe shots. This is the difference between the really good player and the ordinary player. Now, any first class player ought to be able to hit the half volley for four runs. It's the great player who hits the good ball either off front or back foot for four runs with a straight-bat shot without taking a chance.❞ **Trevor Bailey**

May duly reached three figures on the fourth morning, but the new ball was taken immediately afterwards and with it Lindwall set about redressing the balance. First he bowled May for 104 and then hit the new batsman, Tyson, (perhaps not the wisest victim to choose for such treatment) on the head. Tyson was able to return later, after an X-ray, only to provide Lindwall with his third wicket of the innings. Archer and Johnston had also both taken three when the innings finally ended at 296, and that only thanks again to a last wicket stand, this time of Appleyard and Statham, which realised 46 runs that were to prove invaluable. Australia needed just 223 runs to win with enough of the fourth day still to go to build a substantial bridgehead.

Either side of the tea interval, though, Tyson and Statham bowled with great fire to remove the openers, so that Burke and Harvey had to hang on to the close at 72 for 2. The target for the final day was 151 with eight wickets in hand – not too steep at all.

Early on that day, however, Tyson did enough to plant doubt in Australian minds. In one over he bowled Burke for 14 and Hole for a duck and Australia were 77 for 4. Benaud stayed with Harvey to add 25 for the fifth wicket, but before lunch he was gone, to Appleyard, for 12. After the interval Tyson and Statham were back with a full head of steam and the cheap wickets of Archer and Davidson. It was 127 for 7 when Lindwall came in.

BOB RICHARDSON

The field changes over as the right hander Lindwall prepares to take strike to Tyson. There's quite a murmur going round the crowd now as they are probably remembering that yesterday Tyson was unfortunate to get in the way of one from Lindwall. He turned his back completely on a ball that got up and, of course we all know that he was knocked out and had to be assisted from the field. Now Tyson moves in, bowls to Lindwall outside the off stump, and it came back at him and Lindwall got an inside edge. The ball just bounced in front of him and goes out towards mid-on. You could hear the gasp going round the crowd then as Lindwall, shaping to play at a ball outside the off stump, found it coming back at him and just

Tyson hit on the head by Lindwall

35

AUSTRALIA
SECOND INNINGS
136-8

Tyson's revenge

AUSTRALIA
SECOND INNINGS
184 all out

found an inside edge and played it out to mid-on. Tyson, bowling to three slips, a gully, a deep third man, extra cover, mid-on, backward square leg and a fine leg deep on the fence. Tyson to Lindwall outside the off stump … and he's bowled him! It came back on him, bowled him, knocked his off stump right out of the ground. Lindwall is out, bowled Tyson for 8. Harvey is 55, 10 sundries, Australia 8 for 136. Well that's the fourth time this morning that Tyson has hit the stumps. His figures are now 5 for 54 and over to Arthur Gilligan.

ARTHUR GILLIGAN

Well that's another well pitched-up ball and I think Tyson has taken a leaf out of Lindwall's book because that's the third time, I would say, that he's hit the stumps with that yorker. Lindwall tried to chop down on it and missed it and his head went up in despair as he saw his off stump knocked back. No, Tyson's done a great job for the England side and this game now has veered, I would say, in England's favour but there's Langley and Johnston to come in, Neil Harvey still there. So don't let anybody imagine that the game's over yet by a long chalk.

Nine runs later, though, it all did look over when Statham bowled wicketkeeper Gil Langley for nought. The last pair needed 78 to win, but one of them was Harvey, who had come in at 4 and now with Bill Johnston fashioned a tenth wicket stand which reached 35 …

BERNARD KERR

Would somebody please pass a nerve tonic? Nine for 184, now Tyson to Johnston. Johnston stands up very straight. Has a look round the field in a real professional style. Here's Tyson to Johnston. Oh … Johnston tries to play the same sort of shot and he's touched it and he's caught by Evans and the match is all over. There's an appeal and Johnston is out, caught Evans, bowled Tyson for 11. England wins, Australia dismissed for 184, the players are congratulating each other, spectators jumping over the fence. Congratulations England, in levelling the Test series, Australia having won in Brisbane. Australia all out for 184 and what a magnificent ovation young Harvey will get, 92 not out as he makes his way towards the gate, I think I'll just keep quiet and let you hear this magnificent ovation for Harvey.

Tyson's 6 for 85 – 10 wickets in the match – had given England victory by 38 runs and cheered up the forthcoming Christmas celebrations, which, just 24 hours earlier had looked likely to be a somewhat muted affair. But for all the joy of victory, one member of the touring party must have been particularly disappointed not to have been part of it.

66That was one of the sad moments in cricket when Alec Bedser was left out of the side. It was an interesting decision because the conditions were absolutely ideal for swing and seam bowling at his pace.

I think that if Alec had played we would have won comfortably because he would have had a field day but lost the series because we wouldn't have got the Tyson/ Statham combination going which really was all important. Alec took it with great sadness obviously, but it was the correct decision and a very bold one.99 **Trevor Bailey**

66He had worked himself into the ground. He was a huge, strong man and far too much labour was thrown on him. He never stinted although his brother, Eric, used sometimes to say, "take it easy, Al." I don't think he ever really did.

May and Cowdrey were part of a fresh vintage. Peter May was a most brilliant on-driver, Colin Cowdrey a superb all-round player. I think, in some ways, Cowdrey was as self-contained and complete a batsman as I've ever seen; I don't think he was ever strained or stretched; I think he never found cricket really difficult.99 **John Arlott**

Alec Bedser (*left*) and shown above with his twin brother, Eric).

Colin Cowdrey

After England's win in Sydney, the series stood at one-all, and New Year's Eve saw long queues at cricket's most capacious arena, the Melbourne Cricket Ground, for the start of the third match of the rubber. For Australia, Ian Johnson and Keith Miller were back, while in the England side, Compton's hand had recovered sufficiently for him to replace Graveney. Hutton won the toss and this time chose Bill Edrich to open with him. Before lunch Miller had removed Edrich, Compton and Hutton, while Lindwall gave May the 25th birthday present of a duck. It was 49 for 4.

Trevor Bailey, ever the man for a crisis, now joined Colin Cowdrey to shore up one end while the strokes flowed from the other. They added 74 for the fifth wicket before Bailey was caught behind for 30, and it was Godfrey Evans who saw Cowdrey to the first of his 22 Test centuries before he was bowled by Johnson for 102. Evans reached 20 as Ron Archer's medium pace mopped up the tail, turning 169 for 5 into 191 all out.

The pitch had already shown signs of variable bounce and on the second day it offered the same service to Tyson and Statham. At 65 for 4 they had run through the top Australian batting, with the exception of Harvey. Appleyard removed him for 31 and added the wicket of Benaud and the clatter of Australian wickets gave England hope. The eighth wicket fell at 151, but the wicketkeeper Len Maddocks and Ian Johnson hung on to the close when they were only three runs behind.

Now came the rest day and one of the great scandals of Test cricket. When the teams came to look at the pitch, which had been a maze of cracks on Saturday night, they found by Monday morning it was smooth and the cracks were closed. Against all the regulations, it had been watered, although this was at first fiercely denied.

The immediate effect was to make batting considerably more comfortable and the Australian tail were able to take their side into a lead of 40, with Maddocks the top scorer, making 47. Brian Statham, who was to appear on this tour to be a foil for Tyson as he did in later years for Trueman, had taken 5 for 60.

The deficit was just cleared when England lost their first wicket. Indeed, batting conditions were now so improved that only three England wickets fell during the day by the close of which they were 159 with Peter May 83 not out. It was a promising enough position for them to feel disappointed with their eventual total of 279 of which May had made 91. Bill Johnston had been the most successful bowler, with 5 for 85. By the close of the fourth day Australia were apparently well on the way to going ahead in the series again at 75 for 2.

The huge crowd that packed into the MCG on the final morning were confident of Australia's ability to score the remaining 165 runs. What they witnessed was the 'Typhoon' in full blast. The previous afternoon he had removed Morris; now, in the first over of the day a spectacular catch by Evans behind the stumps accounted for Harvey and not long after, the night watchman, Benaud, was bowled for 22. It was the start of a rout during which six wickets fell for 24 runs to bring the last pair together before lunch.

MICHAEL CHARLTON

Tyson to carry on and bowl this time to Ian Johnson to two slips, a gully, third man, cover, mid off, the off side field. Australia 9 for 110, needing 240 to win and Tyson bowls to Johnson and he bowls to him on the off stump and Johnson gets him down through the gully, steers it down there, Wardle coming in, they take one, one's all they'll get. Wardle comes to the ball and there's his left arm return going into Evans' gloves now near the stumps. Johnson 4, Johnston yet to score, this gives Bill Johnston the strike, Australia 9 for 111.

Well now, Bill Johnston moves into the wicket, and you can see this enormous piece of plaster that covers the inside edge of his bat and which I saw last night was severely marked in red along the edge, and Tyson bowls to Bill Johnston now and this ball beats him just outside the off stump.

There's an appeal for a catch behind and he's gone! A great catch by Evans diving right across, Evans is rolling round on the ground and Bill Johnston is out, caught Evans bowled Tyson for no score and Australia all out for 111, Tyson's final figures being 7 for 27.

Brian Statham

AUSTRALIA SECOND INNINGS 111 all out

39

JOHNNY MOYES

During this session Australia lost eight wickets for 36 runs and that's one of the most remarkable pieces of cricket in the history of the Test match and the man who did the job was once again Tyson. Now, Tyson, this morning, came up the hill which doesn't help him and he attacked all the time. He's a great-hearted fellow and, well, you've heard us say so often, the admiration we have for this chap. He can keep going as long as you like. He will keep going. He gives his last ounce that he's got in him. He'll race round the outfield and chase the ball and then come back and bowl fast and he's got a mighty good helper in Statham. Those two are a great attacking pair. They work well together, both of them going at the stumps all the time, and since the Brisbane Test match they've learnt a good deal, I think, from watching Lindwall and Miller because, whereas in Brisbane they didn't bowl any yorkers at all, they fire them in fairly regularly now.

❝On that tour I think Tyson was the fastest thing I've ever seen. Frank was a close friend of mine; we used to room together; we used to go out looking at bookshops together; we got on very well together then and afterwards. I admired him terrifically as a fast bowler, he saw fast bowling as something on which he could spend himself. He was at my house when he got the news by telegram that he'd passed his university degree. He suddenly went out of the house and came back with a bottle of champagne and said, "We'll drink this." I said, "Come on, Frank, what's it all about?"
He said, "I've passed my degree, which means I don't have to save myself; I can bowl as fast as ever I can, so long as I want to bowl as fast as ever I can, and then I can go away and earn a peaceful living." If he had had to make a living out of the game I think he would have been too shrewd to have gone on spending himself like that.❞

John Arlott

❝After Brisbane, where he took not many for plenty he shortened his run which made the crucial difference. He had been charging in from between 25 and 30 yards, which was a terrible run-up. It was spectacular but, if everything didn't go exactly right, which frequently it didn't, he ended up all over the place. So he cut down to 8 or 9 paces, gained a lot more control and didn't lose any pace. If you run 25 yards with arms and legs going everywhere it's much more difficult to get your timing right than it is from 13 yards and this, to my mind, transformed him from a fast bowler into a very good fast bowler. His secret was pace, nothing more, not movement. I think the best description of his pace was given to me by Arthur Morris when we went out together for a drive on a Sunday. He summed it up very accurately. Arthur reckoned that the difference between Brian Statham, who was fast, and me at fast medium, was the same difference again between Statham and Tyson. And Staham was quick.

Tyson's solution was simply to bowl faster than anyone else. He was frighteningly quick. I suppose there have been perhaps three occasions watching Michael Holding, when I've seen bowling as fast as that.

With Tyson, we're talking about excessive speed. I remember him over here on holiday about twenty years later playing in a charity match. He bowled a bouncer to Keith Fletcher and Fletcher told me afterwards: "that's about the quickest ball I've seen this summer.**❞** **Trevor Bailey**

Clockwise: Tyson, Statham and Bailey

From being 1-nil down, England were now 2-1 up and only a draw in one of the two remaining Tests was needed to retain the Ashes. When Ian Johnson chose to bat on the first day at Adelaide, the temperature was in the hundreds.

Hutton spared his bowlers by using them in short bursts, but there was no early breakthrough on a slow scoring morning. Tyson did manage to get Morris just after lunch with some unexpected lift, but Colin McDonald, who had displaced Favell, fell to the off spin of Appleyard, or, more likely to relief at the introduction of spin, but, mostly, it was a first day of attritional defence and only two more wickets fell: Burke and Harvey to Tyson and Bailey. It was 161 for 4 at the close.

Before the arrival of the second new ball next day, Appleyard gave England the bonus wickets of the two overnight batsmen, Miller and Benaud, and it was 182 for 6. The new ball, in the hands of Tyson and Bailey, brought the end of Archer and Davidson to make it 229 for 8 and, on a perfect pitch, put England right in charge. But Maddocks and Johnson, who had performed minor heroics for the ninth wicket in Melbourne, now staged a repeat performance in Adelaide by adding 92 to pull Australia back into the reckoning. Maddocks was eventually run out for 69 and Johnson gave Bailey his third wicket as the Australian innings ended on the second afternoon at 323.

In reply England at last enjoyed a healthy opening stand from Hutton and Edrich, who were still together at the close, but Edrich went early on the third morning, which brought in Peter May.

CHARLES FORTUNE
In comes Benaud to May. Oh! He has May in trouble there right back on his stumps. I don't quite know why Maddocks lifted the bails. Maddocks lifted the bails but May at the moment the bails were lifted had both feet inside the crease. He was coming back towards the stumps rather than going forward but Maddocks perhaps with the joy of being out there in the middle too much for him, lifted those bails. Benaud in, comes in to May. May beaten by this and he's caught, he's caught at first slip a lovely catch by Archer, caught at first slip.

May caught Archer bowled Benaud, 1 run. England 2 for 63, and this morning they have lost two wickets and what valuable wickets!

It was a disappointing start for Hutton to observe from the other end, but now he found support from Cowdrey who picked his shots as he put together a half century and their partnership mounted towards three figures...

 **CHARLES FORTUNE**
Johnston in to Hutton. Hutton off the back foot, hits this firmly. Cowdrey turns and gets back inside the crease as Bill Johnston fields. Cowdrey of course, does tend to back up pretty vigorously and he was certainly backing up that time. Johnston bowling, Hutton hits this hard ... and is caught.

He's caught at short leg, caught at forward short leg by Davidson. Hutton out for 80. Hutton caught Davidson, bowled Bill Johnston off rather a bad ball. Hutton lay back to hit that through mid-wicket, Davidson backed away, but kept his eye on the ball and then the ball came gently to him and he hugged it to his midriff. Altogether that was something of a comedy of errors but Davidson, at any rate, hung on to the catch. So Hutton caught Davidson, bowled Bill Johnston 80. England 3 for 162, partnership 99.

Now Compton joined Cowdrey in a fourth wicket stand which added 70, of which Compton had the lion's share with 44, passing, along the way, his previous highest score in Australia, which he was to exceed comfortably in the next Test. But at 232 both Cowdrey and Compton fell to Miller and Davidson. Now Bailey and Evans came together in a partnership of 50 in which Evans seemed determined to step up the tempo of the innings on the fourth morning.

Both men reached thirty and Wardle made 23 so that, with eight wickets down, England took the lead and stretched it to 18 runs.

If another Tyson blitz was expected, Hutton had a surprise up his sleeve as he now gave Bob Appleyard a long bowl and was amply rewarded with three wickets by the close of play. On the fifth morning, though, he was back to the demolition squad of Tyson and Statham...

ENGLAND
FIRST INNINGS
63-2

ENGLAND
FIRST INNINGS
162-3

Denis Compton

ENGLAND
FIRST INNINGS
257-5

43

**AUSTRALIA
SECOND INNINGS
69-4**

Brian Statham

CHARLES FORTUNE

So, Statham in to McDonald. Bowling, McDonald struck on the pad. No appeal from Statham. McDonald turned, trying to play that ball just backward of square leg, but the ball was a bit too quick for him had him on the pads, well outside the leg stump. Now, people still moving into their seats. Not the biggest crowd by any manner of means that we've seen here but a truly tip-top morning for the cricket. Statham's third ball ... he bowls, full toss and he's bowled McDonald. Well now there is tragedy for you, a full toss that's clean bowled McDonald. McDonald goes with the third ball of the morning. Australia 4 for 69, McDonald 29.

Only another seven runs were added before Statham also bowled Miller for 14. At 77, Tyson had Benaud lbw for 1, and, two runs later, Statham did the same to Maddocks. Alan Davidson scored 23 before Wardle had him lbw, but with two more tail-end wickets for Tyson, Australia were soon out, for the second successive Test match, for the dreaded 'Nelson' – 111.

So England needed only 94 to win, but Keith Miller, without his old comrade-in-arms, the injured Lindwall, set about showing that it was no formality. In a fine spell of bowling he removed Hutton, Edrich and Cowdrey to reduce England to 18 for 3, but, even though Bill Johnston also nabbed two wickets, England at last got themselves to the brink of the victory which would secure the Ashes ...

ALAN McGILVRAY

So there's only three runs now wanted. Five wickets down for 91. Compton is 34, Evans has not yet scored, sundries are 7 and Miller to bowl. He's now bowling to Evans. Evans turns, pushes it away on the off side goes looking for one. There's a scream as Evans scampers up the wicket and Benaud came in but again there was no danger of a run out. He was only joking but his scream caused Benaud to misfield the ball. Evans, just scampering down the wicket, was well in control of the situation and there was no chance of being run out. Evans now facing Miller. And he cuts it down through the gully. There's one in it. He's looking for two here and McDonald's coming to the ball now and he's going to be close! No it's too slow, and Evans is too fast for that. He went right through with that second run. McDonald was coming in, a little slow in getting to it and Evans, quite fast up the wicket, and now the scores are level. Five for 93, Compton 34, Evans 2. Scores level. It's a tie as it stands with five wickets in hand. One run wanted for victory. Miller moves in and bowls to Evans. It's hit high and hit for four. Gone away to the boundary for four and it's four runs, 5 wickets for 97 and England win the match by five wickets.

The crowd swarming all over the ground now to congratulate the players. They're all round Compton and they're running all over the ground to add their congratulations. And now I would like to introduce Len Hutton. And I would say to you, on behalf of the Australian listeners and the broadcasting team, Len, heartiest congratulations on winning the Ashes and for the superb part you played in handling your side, and the job you've done. I have admired your captaincy, your work and it's been wonderful having you here. Very well done old chap and I'm delighted to see that you're going to give your good thoughts to our public over here.

LEN HUTTON

Thank you very much indeed Alan. It is a great moment here for me today. Godfrey Evans has just hit the winning hit and at this moment the crowd are surging on to the field giving the players as they come off a wonderful reception. At this moment, of course, we are feeling pretty tired and I really don't know what to say except this morning we saw some magnificent fast bowling by Tyson and Brian Statham and then this afternoon when we started our innings we saw a magnificent spell of bowling from Keith Miller who, I think, is the finest bowler with a new ball that I know. He bowled magnificently and he gave us all quite a lot of worries for some time this afternoon. I know all the team are very, very happy indeed at the result as I know all you will be at home. Thank you very much.

It was wholly appropriate that Len Hutton should be on hand in the radio commentary box at that moment, because this was a very personal triumph for him in winning the series in no small measure as the result of his own strategy.

Frank Tyson

45

❝Len Hutton was dour, but a very shrewd tactician, the type I always wanted to play under. He wasn't a leader from the front. He wasn't a "come on chaps, lets charge" type. He let you get on with your job. He was far more impressed by fast than slow bowling, because he played slow bowling better, if anything, than he played fast bowling … So he did have a tendency to put great emphasis on the quicks and, of course, if you look at the modern game you realise they are pretty important. It was a brief he always held. Hutton was a master batsman and beautiful to watch. Unlike Boycott, he could make the forward defensive look attractive. His off-drive was very graceful, something to remember. He was marvellous on bad wickets. Len had a run machine ticking inside him – he loved batting. If I scored 50, I would be happy, but Len needed to score a hundred because there was a tendency to regard anything less than a hundred as failure.❞ **Trevor Bailey**

The final six-day Test of the series was ruined by rain which did not allow any play until the fourth afternoon. Tom Graveney made 111 and Lindwall taking the wickets of Evans and Bailey. He became the first to take 100 in Anglo-Australian Tests as England rapidly ran up 371 for 7 declared by tea on the fifth day. Although McDonald made 72, Australian wickets fell at regular intervals, chiefly to Appleyard, so that they were all out on the final afternoon for 221 and with the match reduced to three days, Hutton enforced the follow-on exactly 150 behind. Only two hours remained, but five wickets fell for 87 – three of them to Wardle and as the last over approached, Australia knew they were safe from a fourth defeat …

JOHNNY MOYES

Well, the game's very nearly over now and we're near the end of the tour, and I don't think that we can do anything else other than congratulate the Englishmen on winning. Their bowlers, Statham and Tyson are a great combination, those two fine young batsmen, Cowdrey and May, Evans' wicketkeeping and that lovely innings by Graveney the other day and Len Hutton as the first professional captain to come out here, and he is going to finish off the tour by bowling the last over. And the crowd is giving him a great reception too, hand claps and cheers all round the ground.

And the captain was to make it an even more suitable end by taking the wicket of Benaud with the last ball of what was, after all, Hutton's tour.

Len Hutton and Denis Compton

*Third Test, Melbourne, 31 December 1954-
5 January 1955*
England won by 128 runs

ENGLAND

*L. Hutton c Hole b Miller	12	lbw b Archer	42
W. J. Edrich c Lindwall b Miller	4	b Johnston	13
P. B. H. May c Benaud b Lindwall	0	b Johnston	91
M. C. Cowdrey b Johnston	102	b Benaud	7
D. C. S. Compton c Harvey b Miller	4	c Maddocks b Archer	23
T. E. Bailey c Maddocks b Johnston	30	not out	24
†T. G. Evans lbw b Archer	20	c Maddocks b Miller	22
J. H. Wardle b Archer	0	b Johnson	38
F. H. Tyson b Archer	6	c Harvey b Johnston	6
J. B. Statham b Archer	3	c Favell b Johnston	0
R. Appleyard not out	1	b Johnston	6
Extras (b9)	9	(b2, lb4, w1)	7
Total	**191**		**279**

AUSTRALIA

L. E. Favell lbw b Statham	25	b Appleyard	30
A. R. Morris lbw b Tyson	3	c Cowdrey b Tyson	4
K. R. Miller c Evans b Statham	7	c Edrich b Tyson	6
R. N. Harvey b Appleyard	31	c Evans b Tyson	11
G. B. Hole b Tyson	11	c Evans b Statham	5
R. Benaud c sub b Appleyard	15	b Tyson	22
R. G. Archer b Wardle	23	b Statham	15
†L. V. Maddocks c Evans b Statham	47	b Tyson	0
R. R. Lindwall b Statham	13	lbw b Tyson	0
*I. W. Johnson not out	33	not out	4
W. A. Johnston b Statham	11	c Evans b Tyson	0
Extras (b7, lb3, nb2)	12	(b1, lb13)	14
Total	**231**		**111**

BOWLING

AUSTRALIA	O	M	R	W		O	M	R	W
Lindwall	13	0	59	1	–	18	3	52	0
Miller	11	8	14	3	–	18	6	35	1
Archer	13.6	4	33	4	–	24	7	50	2
Benaud	7	0	30	0	–	8	2	25	1
Johnston	12	6	26	1	–	24.5	2	25	5
Johnson	11	3	20	1	–	8	2	25	1
ENGLAND									
Tyson	21	2	68	2	–	12.3	1	27	7
Statham	16.3	0	60	5	–	11	1	38	2
Bailey	9	1	33	0	–	3	0	14	0
Appleyard	11	3	38	2	–	4	1	17	1
Wardle	6	0	20	1	–	1	0	1	0

ENGLAND fall of wickets
FIRST INNINGS: 1-14, 2-21, 3-29, 4-41, 5-115, 6-169, 7-181, 8-181, 9-190.
SECOND INNINGS: 1-40, 2-96, 3-128, 4-173, 5-185, 6-211, 7-257, 8-273, 9-273.
AUSTRALIA fall of wickets
FIRST INNINGS: 1-15, 2-38, 3-43, 4-65, 5-92, 6-115, 7-134, 8-151, 9-205.
SECOND INNINGS: 1-23, 2-57, 3-77, 4-86, 5-87, 6-97, 7-98, 9-110.

First Test at Brisbane, November 26 –
December 1
Australia won by an innings and 154 runs
Australia 601-8 dec (Harvey 162, Morris
153, Lindwall 64*, Hole 57); England 190
(Bailey 88) and 257 (Edrich 88).

Second Test at Sydney, December 17-22
England won by 38 runs.
England 154 and 296 (May 104, Cowdrey
54); Australia 228 and 184 (Harvey 92*,
Tyson 6-85).

Fourth Test at Adelaide, January 28 –
February 2
England won by 5 wickets
Australia 323 (Maddocks 69) and 111;
England 341 (Hutton 80, Cowdrey 79) and
97-5.

Fifth Test at Sydney, February 25 –
March 3
Match drawn
England 371-7 dec (Graveney 111,
Compton 84, May 79, Bailey 72); Australia
221 (McDonald 72, Wardle 5-79) and
118-6.

AUSTRALIA IN ENGLAND 1956

The Second Test, **Lord's,** *June 21-26*
The Third Test, **Headingley,** *July 12-17*
The Fourth Test, **Old Trafford,** *July 26-31*
Commentators **Rex Alston, John Arlott and Michael Charlton**
Summarisers **E. W. Swanton, Jack Fingleton and George Duckworth**

The 1956 Australians

Keith Miller, Cyril Washbrook and Jim Laker are the heroes of this story, though other great names have their parts to play. It was a wet summer – one of the wettest, in fact – but three Test matches were finished.

England had won the Ashes back in 1953 and they started this defence of them at Trent Bridge in early June, led by Peter May who had taken over a year earlier. The Australians arrived at Lord's for the Second Test in some disarray. They had yet to beat a county and, during the First Test, had lost Ray Lindwall and Alan Davidson with leg injuries, which brought Pat Crawford into the side for his first Test.

For England, Tyson was unavailable, but an attack of Statham, Trueman and Bailey looked likely to give them the edge, especially with Laker and Wardle to follow.

Yet Colin McDonald and Jim Burke gave Australia their best start for 26 years, with a stand of 137 which only ended as tea approached on the first day. Trevor Bailey made the breakthrough with the wicket of McDonald and then, three balls later, had the new batsman, Neil Harvey, caught behind for nought.

After such an encouraging start the Australians must have been disappointed with the eventual total of 285 when they were all out on the second afternoon.

Even that had owed a great deal to a sixth wicket stand of 54 between Ron Archer and the new cap, Ken Mackay, who made 38.

Archer was soon burdened with more responsibility when, in his fifth over, Crawford pulled a thigh muscle and was out of the match. Thus, Archer was sharing the new ball with Miller, who was now the only spearhead. The situation brought the best out of Miller.

66Miller was mercurial. He had a very steep delivery and a very high, easy action. You were never quite sure what he was going to do with the ball, but he could be quick.99

Trevor Bailey

66He was a great man for rising to occasions and he did so here. He was a very genuine all-rounder and capable of being great as both bowler and batsman — a Botham type of player. On the previous tour in 1953 particularly, he had really been required as a batsman but had had to bowl.99   **John Arlott**

66Keith Miller was a magnificent cricketer. As a bowler, he was an enigma. You never knew what the bloke was going to do. He'd run up and bowl quick — and I mean quick — then he'd bowl a googly, then an off-cutter, then a slower ball, then a bouncer … and they were all difficult to spot.. During a game against MCC I once saw him bowl David Sheppard with a googly … using the new ball!

In that sense he had a cavalier approach and was always full of fun on the field, but when Lindwall was missing he would shoulder the responsibility of carrying the attack with the utmost seriousness. His attitude was that he played to win, but if they lost, they lost. He would never moan or whinge about it. He'd try to knock your block off on the field but, afterwards, in the bar, he'd be the first to buy you a drink.99

Fred Trueman

Lord's was a favourite ground for Keith Miller and this time he quickly showed what he could do on its green pitch by having Peter Richardson, in his second Test, caught behind and then bowling Graveney. England were 32 for 2. Mackay had been promoted to the role of third seamer and soon he had Cowdrey well caught by Benaud above

49

his head at gully. At the close of a tense second day, England were 74 for 3. Miller started the third day by removing Watson cheaply, but Bailey came in to provide the perfect foil for May. Benaud made the breakthrough, bowling May with a top-spinner and having Evans stumped immediately. Now the most important wicket for Australia to capture was Bailey's and Miller obliged, to start and then finish the final slide. From 161 for 6, England were all out for 171, 114 behind.

The life in the pitch which had been exploited by Miller was there, too, for Fred Trueman after Bailey had separated the openers by having McDonald superbly caught in the gully by Cowdrey. Bowling really fast, Trueman sent back Burke, Harvey and Burge and when Bailey had Archer caught behind it seemed that Australia, at 79 for 5, had failed to press home their advantage. The flamboyant Miller came in to join the dogged, phlegmatic 'Slasher' Mackay and set about redressing the balance. After a rest, Trueman was brought back for a final burst on that Saturday evening ...

JOHN ARLOTT

Mackay not out 9, Miller not out 28 and Trueman is here again, bowls to Miller, a bouncer and Miller carts that away on the leg side and Richardson at long leg has got a mighty long run for it. He did not quite middle it ... they run a comfortable two.

112 for 5 and the statisticians may rub their hands at this stand. It is now worth 33 of which Miller has scored 30. "Dear sir, is this a record?" In fact I understand it is not. Hornby and Barlow, I believe, for Lancashire years ago, Barlow had 1 out of the first 52 and Hornby the rest. I do not go in for statistics but that is history. Anything connected with Lancashire cricket is history. And the lead now is 126. And Trueman comes in, bowls to Miller, Miller gropes and Evans has caught him most gloriously! And now all round the ground, the entire crowd standing to this man again. Well with two receptions like that — three in fact — in one day at Lords, Miller should go to bed tonight a happy man. Men have made more than 30 runs in Tests here but not so many of them have made them as handsomely as that, 112 for 6, Miller caught Evans, bowled

Fiery Fred

Trueman. And Trueman, after a few years in the wilderness as a Test fast bowler, back right in the picture with now 4 for 35 and 4 wickets as good as those of Burke, Harvey, Burge, Miller. What a good bag!

The wicket of Miller brought in Richie Benaud, who survived a confident appeal from Trueman for caught behind before the close of that third day, at which point it seemed anybody's game.

On Monday, though, Benaud's batting took the game right away from England. He made 97 of a seventh wicket partnership of 117 with Mackay and fell to a skied catch as he tried to get his hundred with a second six off Trueman with the new ball. Mackay fell to Statham for 31, scored at an average of seven runs an hour and Bailey polished off the innings. England's target was 372 in just over $8\frac{1}{2}$ hours.

Archer, rejoicing in a rare opportunity to use the new ball, removed Richardson and Miller sent back Graveney before the end of the fourth day's play, when England were 72 for 2. The task for the final day was surely now not so daunting as that facing Bailey and Watson three years before on this ground but Watson was soon bowled by a full toss from Miller. Cowdrey had fallen back on dour defence, but after a three hour innings Benaud had him lbw for 27. May and Bailey added 51 for the fifth wicket, but the ending of that stand just before lunch ended England's hopes. May again was the only England batsman to pass 50, but Miller accounted for him for 53. The gate was wide open and Australia, led by Miller, completed a 185-run victory. Keith Miller took the only 10-wicket match haul of his Test career and Gil Langley's nine victims behind the stumps remained a Test record until 1980. Enough had been seen of Miller to discourage English groundsmen from preparing any more green pitches that season.

Before the Third Test at Headingley the selectors, chaired by Gubby Allen, sprang a surprise when they chose one of their own number, the 41-year-old Cyril Washbrook, who had not played a Test since early 1951 in New Zealand.

66 The selectors had some brainwaves in that series, and I think they were given the credit for them at the time. 99 **John Arlott**

66 It was another Gubby Allen ploy and, by golly, it worked. Washbrook must have been very close to lbw before he scored, but then he played magnificently. 99 **Brian Johnston**

Cyril Washbrook (*right*) proved an inspired choice. Later in the series, the selectors had equal success with Compton

ENGLAND
FIRST INNINGS
203-3

Washbrook came in to face something of a crisis at 17 for 3 to join Peter May, who had won the toss and then seen Ron Archer remove Richardson, Cowdrey and the debutant, Alan Oakman, for 9 runs between them. Although Lindwall was back, Miller had a knee injury which prevented him bowling. May and Washbrook set about the business of recovery. They succeeded admirably. ...

MICHAEL CHARLTON
Three for 195, England, with May 93 and Washbrook 89. Mackay again to bowl from the Pavilion End to May ... outside the off stump and short and May lays back and it's a lovely shot! Away through the covers off the back foot. What a beautiful stroke. It gives them no time — and they're fairly deep on the off side. Miller at cover, Harvey at extra couldn't move to it. Through to the fence for four.

Now, Mackay bowls to May ... on the leg stump and May cracks that through mid wicket. There's his hundred, I think, it's going like a rocket to the fence for four. Burge is after it, but he won't get it. Four runs and there's May's hundred!

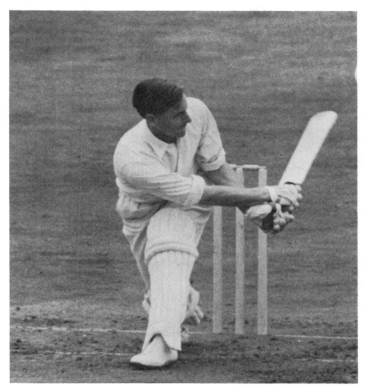

Five minutes before the close of that first day, May was out, caught at fine leg off Johnson for 101. The fourth wicket had put on 187 and changed the face of the game. Washbrook went in that evening after his first day of Test cricket for five and a half years, 90 not out, with England 204 for 5. The next day, Washbrook took the first half hour to add two and then with two shots off Benaud, reached 98 ...

MICHAEL CHARLTON
Washbrook two runs short of what will be a thoroughly good hundred, if he gets it. Missed twice, but what a knock this chap's played. And Benaud bowls to Washbrook ... short, he goes back — he's rapped on the pads — an appeal for lbw — and he's out! ... Washbrook, lbw to Benaud for 98. Well, no-one would have begrudged this chap a hundred. He's being applauded by the Australians as he leaves the field. He played back and he was plumb in front. England 5 for 226, Lock not out 10 and listen to this applause as Washbrook leaves the field. ... A great ovation ...

66I suppose to a whole generation of people Peter May *(left)* is nothing other than the former chairman of the England selectors. It's a pity because he was a bit of a god-like figure really. He was the epitome of what you might think of an English gentleman. He was always immaculate — everything was as white as white — and he was such a marvellous batsman. It's very difficult to fault him as a batsman. He was tough on the field as captain, very tough. By that I mean he'd say what he wanted, but, if you then went to interview him after the game you simply could not get anything out of him at all. It was always: "the boys did well".

He played the quicks and the slows equally well and he did have all the strokes. I think he was tremendous and it's very sad that people now just think of him as rather a laughable chairman of selectors ... but he never was a very good communicator.**99**
Brian Johnston

ENGLAND
FIRST INNINGS
226-5

May and Washbrook

Benaud followed up that wicket with those of Insole and Lock. Bailey and Evans added 53 for the eighth wicket, of which Evans contributed 40, before Lindwall wrapped up the innings with the last three wickets. England were all out for 325 in the middle of the second afternoon.

Fast bowling failed to make a major impact on the game, but Trueman did his bit by taking the important wicket of McDonald in the first over. After that, Laker and Lock set to work on a dry, dusty pitch and, despite staunch resistance from Burke, 41, took the next five wickets – three to Laker, two to Lock. When bad light stopped play a quarter of an hour early, Australia were 81 for 6. That light was the advance shadow of rain which washed out Saturday's play completely.

When the match resumed, 75 minutes late on Monday morning, it was anything but dry and dusty in the middle and Miller and Benaud, the heroes of Lord's, were able to carry their partnership to 73 before the sun emerged to aid the drying process and, with it, Benaud holed out in the deep off Laker for 30. Only one more run was added in the innings. Laker also claimed Miller for 41. He finished with 5 for 58 and Lock 4 for 41. Australia were all out for 143 and Peter May invited them to follow on.

Again Trueman started England off by sending back McDonald, this time with only 10 on the board, but again everyone knew it was just a prelude to Laker and Lock. At 45, Laker bowled Burke for 16 and in came Miller, promoted in the order, to join Harvey. Together they battled through to the end of the fourth day, with the ball turning and the fielders hovering close in. It was 93 for 2 and the chance was there to save the game.

Next morning the big right-hander and the dapper left-hander took their third wicket stand past 60. …

🏆 JOHN ARLOTT
107 for 2 and Laker again comes in — bowls to Harvey … straightens that, but Harvey turns it out on the leg side and there's his fifty. All the England team are joining in. A fifty without the usual pleasures, but a magnificently played one. Australia, then, this morning 108 for 2. Harvey's 50 came in three hours 23 minutes, with 5 fours, Miller 26. And

*now we'll watch this ball from Laker from the Grandstand
End to Miller as soon as he settles. Two short legs. Laker in …
bowls … he straightens that … he turns it, and Miller is
caught by Trueman beautifully one handed, going down to his
right off a ball that turned sharply. And that's Miller caught
Trueman, bowled Laker 26. Australia 108 for 3.*

Miller had batted for nearly $2\frac{1}{2}$ hours for 26 and it had
included two sixes. It was the crucial wicket and Australia's
last 7 wickets eventually crumbled for 20 runs. Harvey was
seventh out to a tumbling caught and bowled by Lock,
who took 3 for 40 – 7 for 81 in the match. But again the
lion's share went to Laker: 6 for 55 for match figures of 11
for 113. It was only a taster for what was to come.

The Australians could not, after that experience,
have been optimistic enough to expect anything other
than a turning pitch for the Fourth Test at Old Trafford. On
the first day, when England had won the toss and Peter
Richardson and Colin Cowdrey were piling up a large
opening partnership, the former Lancashire and England
wicket-keeper George Duckworth, who knew Old
Trafford better than most, gave his view of the pitch from
the commentary box …

GEORGE DUCKWORTH
*I can't walk a yard on the ground without somebody
wanting to know what's wrong with this Old Trafford
wicket. One hundred and seventy for none, nothing wrong with
the wicket at the moment. I wouldn't want to be a pace bowler
on there, but spin bowlers, I think, should get something out of
it in a day or two. It's made for batting today, certainly.*

REX ALSTON
*A good toss to win then, as Lindwall comes in and bowls
a fresh over to Cowdrey, who plays forward and the ball
is fielded by mid-off. We have been talking, George, quite a lot
about the showers of dust that are flying as the bowler delivers
the ball, which is a bit disconcerting, but I don't think we have
seen very many puffs of dust where the ball pitches, have we?*

GEORGE DUCKWORTH
*No, the wicket has had a lot of marl applied to it since the
start of this season, that's why it's a different colour from
the rest of the middle.*

REX ALSTON
Yes. Lindwall again running in, full sail, down wind. Comes in, bowls to Cowdrey. Cowdrey goes for it and he's out! … a lifting ball. Caught Maddocks, bowled Lindwall for 80. England 174, the crowd stand up and I'll stop talking while you hear what they think of Cowdrey's innings.

GEORGE DUCKWORTH
Well, the best opening partnership I've seen for a long, long time by anybody, England or opponents, and I think that the fact that there was not a lot of pace in the wicket meant that these chaps were able to play strokes, and we've seen some wonderful shots played this morning. After two overs, the Australian attacking field had been altered to a completely defensive field and that gives you an idea how the Australians sized up that they were in for a rough time in the field today.

**ENGLAND
FIRST INNINGS
174-1**

Richardson went on to reach his first Test century not long afterwards, but Benaud had him caught behind by Maddocks for 104.

The Reverend David Sheppard, who had been the selectors' surprise choice this time, even though he had given up full time cricket in favour of the Church and had played only four innings for Sussex in the season, had come in at number three. He proved to be another inspired selection, as he was joined now by his captain in a third wicket stand of 93, which only ended towards the close of play when Benaud got one to turn and lift sharply.

By the close, England were 307 for 3, and although the pitch was dry and dusty the Australian bowlers were unable to exploit it.

On the second morning England continued in breezy vein, particularly jaunty wicket-keeper Godfrey Evans, who made 47 out of a stand of 62 in only 29 minutes with Sheppard, who was still there when the tenth man, Lock, came in …

E. W. SWANTON
Lock is looking rather more pleased because that one there from Benaud turned some six inches or so. I don't suppose he's worried about how the wicket's playing, although he'll obviously want to stay there until Sheppard gets his hundred. He's certainly earned his hundred, hasn't he?

The Reverend David Sheppard

ENGLAND
FIRST INNINGS
429-8

REX ALSTON
Oh, indeed. And now Johnson runs in from the Stretford End and he bowls very short indeed and Sheppard ... Oh, a beautiful late cut! It's gone past Archer ... I don't think Mackay can catch it ... The ball is trickling ever so slowly to the boundary ... and it's there! And Sheppard's got his hundred. And now the spectators have all stood up to applaud him. Johnson and several other Australians went and congratulated him. Sheppard 101.

The England innings continued until shortly after lunch, when they were all out for 459, their highest total against Australia since 1948 and made in only 491 minutes. But the real drama of the match was still to come. The Australian openers, McDonald and Burke, found themselves facing the spin of Laker and Lock early on, but they made a steady enough start of 48. The change came when May switched Laker to the Stretford End, from where he dismissed McDonald for 32 and Harvey for 0 to send Australia back into the pavilion at tea with 62 for 2 on the board.

England tightened their grip on the match from the ball after the interval.

AUSTRALIA
FIRST INNINGS
62-3

MICHAEL CHARLTON
Play is about to start. It's Lock from the Manchester end to bowl to Burke. Left arm round the wicket to a slip, a gully, a short third man, cover, extra cover, mid-off, mid-on, forward short leg, short fine leg. Lock bowls to Burke ... Burke forward — he's caught here at first slip by Cowdrey! He went forward to it, it turned and he edged it. Cowdrey dived to his right and Burke is out. And Australia's third wicket falls at 62.

That, to his increasing frustration, was to be the only wicket that Lock would take in the match. But it opened the floodgates for Laker. In 35 minutes after tea that Friday, the last 8 Australian wickets fell for 22 runs. Laker, polishing off the rest, finished with 9 for 37 and with more than an hour of the second day to go, Australia were following on, 375 behind. Before the close, they had seen McDonald retire hurt on 11, with a knee injury, and Harvey bag a "pair" – to Laker of course. The rumblings about unfair preparation of the pitch grew overnight.

Laker and Lock

The rain was to come down on Saturday and only three quarters of an hour's play was possible. That was time enough for Burke to fall into Laker's leg trap. Not much more play was achieved on Monday and so that when the final day started, even at 84 for 2, Australia had a chance of saving the game. Play started ten minutes late with the pitch now damp and too slow for the bowlers. McDonald had resumed his innings on Saturday afternoon and he and Ian Craig fought determinedly through to lunch at 112 for 2. But, just before that, the sun appeared and the spinners immediately achieved some sharp turn. In nine overs after the interval Laker removed Craig for 38 then Miller, Mackay and Archer all for nought. It was 130 for 6. But McDonald and Benaud lasted the remaining 75 minutes to tea. …

MICHAEL CHARLTON

Well, it's Laker to resume after tea and from round the wicket from the Stretford End, he comes in and bowls to McDonald, McDonald back and he turns that one into the leg trap, may have let it run off his pad to Oakman at backward short leg. McDonald 89, Benaud 15, Australia 6 for 181. Laker, round the wicket to McDonald, comes in and bowls further up, McDonald back here. There are appeals for a catch … and he's caught in the leg trap! Caught by Oakman, as he played back to that ball. It ran from the bat to the pad. And that's the one they wanted. McDonald caught Oakman, bowled Laker for 89 and Australia are 7 for 181. Before anyone says a word, listen to the applause this boy gets as he walks off the field. What a job he's done.

AUSTRALIA
SECOND INNINGS
181-7

Now, in just under three hours, Laker and Lock had the task of taking the last three Australian wickets. The ball was turning more quickly than ever, but Benaud and Lindwall managed a stand of 17 before Laker bowled Benaud for 18. Two wickets to go …

JOHN ARLOTT
Two hundred and three for 8 Australia. 203 for 8.
Lindwall 8, Johnson 1 and Laker comes in again to Lindwall. He's in, bowls, Lindwall plays it on the leg side and is caught. There's an appeal and he's out. Caught Lock, bowled Laker. Lindwall caught Lock, bowled Laker, 8. Well that's 18 wickets — the most wickets taken by a bowler in a Test match. Eighteen wickets for Laker.

AUSTRALIA
SECOND INNINGS
203-9

The wicket of Lindwall gave Laker his record *(right)*

The tools of Laker's trade *(below)*

JOHN ARLOTT
Old Trafford has redeemed itself with a last hour of flawless sunshine. Laker comes in again, hair flopping, bowls to Maddocks, it turns and Laker appeals and he's out lbw and Laker's taken all ten! The first man to congratulate him is Ian Johnson and England have won by an innings and 170 and Laker has taken all ten wickets for 53 in the second innings.

Now here's the avenue forming up for Laker, as May pushes him ahead to go in first into the pavilion. All the members standing, waving their scorecards, standing up on the balcony, leaning down and applauding him. He runs up the pavilion steps in through that crowd and is followed into the pavilion. And there are friends of mine who were not going to come today, they thought it would rain. Well it did look as if it was going to rain. They missed a very great piece of bowling.

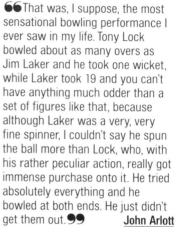

❝That was, I suppose, the most sensational bowling performance I ever saw in my life. Tony Lock bowled about as many overs as Jim Laker and he took one wicket, while Laker took 19 and you can't have anything much odder than a set of figures like that, because although Laker was a very, very fine spinner, I couldn't say he spun the ball more than Lock, who, with his rather peculiar action, really got immense purchase onto it. He tried absolutely everything and he bowled at both ends. He just didn't get them out.**❞** **John Arlott**

❝It was a classic case of knowing it was going to turn before we started. I said afterwards, turning to Peter Richardson as we left the field, "We have taken part in something which will never happen again. No one will ever take 19 wickets in a Test match again." It didn't make sense then and it still doesn't. The most remarkable thing was not that Laker took 19 wickets but that Lock took only one. And the reason, of course, was temperament. The more wickets Laker took, the more Lock tried and tried and the faster and faster he bowled. Meanwhile Jim just carried on putting the ball on the spot, and letting the pitch do the work.**❞** **Trevor Bailey**

The final wicket *(above)* and the celebration *(left)*

Laker's swollen spinning finger

66 If Johnny Wardle had been at the other end there is no way that Laker would have taken 19 wickets. And it wasn't a question of generosity — they were fiercely competitive when it came to wickets. It was unbelievable. But an English county side on that pitch would have played better than the Australians.

They thought they'd been done. They thought they'd been stuffed. Well, they had been. 99

Trevor Bailey

66 There was a marvellous moment at the end. Laker had just taken the final wicket — and he just swung round, took his sweater from the umpire and walked off as if nothing had happened. I think someone patted him on the back, but there was nothing more than that. When he got to the pavilion they let him walk through and I had to go very quickly to fetch him for a television interview. I remember going to the dressing room and they were all popping champagne corks. In the corner was old Jim drinking what looked like orange juice, absolutely quiet. I think he was in a bit of a daze and hadn't quite realised what he had done. Later, he stopped at a pub on the journey back to London and the television was showing the highlights of his performance which was the talk of the clientele. He was not recognised by anyone in the pub. 99 **Brian Johnston**

BOWLERS	RUNS EACH OVER																				OVRS	MDNS	RUNS	WKTS
	1	2	3	4	5	6	7	8	9	10	11	12	13	14	15	16	17	18	19	20				
LAKER	M		3w4					M			W		M		2			MM		M				
		M		MM4		MM	WWW	M			WM		2		M									
		M		W				MW		M	w										51.2	23	53	10

Laker's record

Fourth Test, Old Trafford, 26-31 July 1956
England won by an innings and 170 runs

ENGLAND

P. E. Richardson c Maddocks b Benaud	104
M. C. Cowdrey c Maddocks b Lindwall	80
Rev. D. S. Sheppard b Archer	113
*P. B. H. May c Archer b Benaud	43
T. E. Bailey b Johnson	20
C. Washbrook lbw b Johnson	6
A. S. M. Oakman c Archer b Johnson	10
†T. G. Evans st Maddocks b Johnson	47
J. C. Laker run out	3
G. A. R. Lock not out	25
J. B. Statham c Maddocks b Lindwall	0
Extras (b2, lb5, w1)	8
Total	**459**

AUSTRALIA

C. C. McDonald c Lock b Laker	32	c Oakman b Laker	89
J. W. Burke c Cowdrey b Lock	22	c Lock b Laker	33
R. N. Harvey b Laker	0	c Cowdrey b Laker	0
I. D. Craig lbw b Laker	8	lbw b Laker	38
K. R. Miller c Oakman b Laker	6	b Laker	0
K. D. Mackay c Oakman b Laker	0	c Oakman b Laker	0
R. G. Archer st Evans b Laker	6	c Oakman b Laker	0
R. Benaud c Statham b Laker	0	b Laker	18
R. R. Lindwall not out	6	c Lock b Laker	8
†L. V. Maddocks b Laker	4	lbw b Laker	2
*I. W. Johnson b Laker	0	not out	1
Extras	0	(b12, lb4)	16
Total	**84**		**205**

BOWLING

AUSTRALIA	O	M	R	W		O	M	R	W
Lindwall	21.3	6	63	2	–				
Miller	21	6	41	0	–				
Archer	22	6	73	1	–				
Johnson	47	10	151	4	–				
Benaud	47	17	123	2	–				
ENGLAND									
Statham	6	3	6	0	–	16	10	15	0
Bailey	4	3	4	0	–	20	8	31	0
Laker	16.4	4	37	9	–	51.2	23	53	10
Lock	14	3	37	1	–	55	30	69	0
Oakman					–	8	3	21	0

ENGLAND fall of wickets
FIRST INNINGS: 1-174, 2-195, 3-288, 4-321, 5-327, 6-339, 7-401, 8-417, 9-458.
AUSTRALIA fall of wickets
FIRST INNINGS: 1-48, 2-48, 3-62, 4-62, 5-62, 6-73, 7-73, 8-78, 9-84.
SECOND INNINGS: 1-28, 2-55, 3-114, 4-124, 5-130, 6-130, 7-181, 8-198, 9-203.

First Test at Trent Bridge, June 7-12
Match drawn
England 217-8 dec (Richardson 81, May 73) and 188-3 dec (Cowdrey 81, Richardson 73); Australia 148 (Harvey 64) and 120-3 (Burke 58*).

Second Test at Lord's, June 21-26
Australia won by 185 runs
Australia 285 (McDonald 78, Burke 65) and 257 (Benaud 97, Trueman 5-90); England 171 (May 63, Miller 5-72) and 186 (May 53, Miller 5-80).

Third Test at Headingley, July 12-17
England won by an innings and 42 runs
England 325 (May 101, Washbrook 98); Australia 143 (Laker 5-58) and 140 (Harvey 69, Laker 6-55).

Fifth Test at The Oval, August 23-28
Match drawn
England 247 (Compton 94, May 83*, Archer 5-53) and 182-3 dec (Sheppard 62); Australia 202 (Miller 61) and 27-5.

AUSTRALIA IN ENGLAND 1961

The Fourth Test, **Old Trafford,** *July 27–August 1, 1961*
Commentators **Rex Alston, John Arlott, Alan McGilvray and Bob Richardson**
Summarisers **Freddie Brown and Jack Fingleton**

The 1961 series was intriguingly balanced when the sides arrived in Manchester, all square, with two to play. Australia's win at Lord's, achieved by Davidson and McKenzie had been cancelled out by Fred Trueman's heroics at Leeds, where, in front of his Yorkshire followers, he routed the enemy almost single-handed. Two extraordinary breakthroughs in spells of 5 for 16 in six overs in the first innings, then 6 for 4 in 45 balls in the second, settled the issue and tied the series. As in those two matches, it seemed at the start of the Fourth Test that fast bowling would rule the day, when Richie Benaud chose to bat after winning the toss. The old firm of Statham and Trueman were in harness with the new ball in overcast conditions, with Jack Flavell, winning his first Test cap, and Ted Dexter in support.

In fact, the weather eventually closed in, to the extent that only $2\frac{1}{2}$ hours play was possible on the first day, by which time Australia were 106 for 4 – two wickets to Statham, one to Trueman, who had induced the uncomfortable and bruised Norman O'Neill to hit his wicket, and Flavell's first Test scalp, Peter Burge. But Bill Lawry was still there next morning, and he went on to make 74, before the persevering Statham had him lbw. He had added 44 for the fifth wicket with Brian Booth and Booth now went on to resist bravely, losing Mackay at 174 …

Brian Statham

BOB RICHARDSON
What a good spell this has been from Statham. Ten overs from a fast bowler and he has not let up all the time, he has been attacking the stumps and bowling intelligently, making that ball move away from Booth … and again Booth is beaten by a ball that lifted a little bit. Booth stands up, and just cannot make this out at the moment.
FREDDIE BROWN   *I don't think Statham can either.*

BOB RICHARDSON
It is amazing. No bowler seems to beat the bat and the stumps quite as much as Statham does. Here is the next one and Booth hits it straight to short forward leg and is caught by Brian Close! Booth is out, caught Close bowled Statham for 46, it is 7 for 185. That gives Statham his fifth wicket of the match.

FREDDIE BROWN
Well that was a very good catch there by Close because he is fielding very near the batsman at short square leg. A matter of eight feet, I should think, and Booth played that one off his leg quite firmly and straight to him.

Dexter now chipped in with the last three wickets, so that before lunch on the second day, England had started their reply to Australia's 190 all out. In the third over they lost Raman Subba Row and, at 43, Dexter. Geoff Pullar put on 111 for the third wicket with his captain Peter May and, though Pullar was bowled by Davidson for 63, by the end of the second day England were three runs behind, with seven wickets in hand.

Just 22 runs on, on Saturday morning, Davidson and McKenzie removed May and Close, May when he was only five runs short of a hundred. But now Ken Barrington, with the aid of first John Murray and then David Allen, made sure that the lead was substantial, with an innings of 78. England, though, did not quite turn the screw as tightly as they must have hoped, with the last four wickets falling for nine runs to Bobby Simpson's leg spin for an eventual total of 367 and a lead of 177.

A century stand between Lawry and Simpson, which lasted well into Monday morning was just the answer Australia needed. And, when Harvey followed Simpson's 51 with his 35, the first two wickets had all but wiped off the deficit. Lawry went on to bat for $4\frac{1}{2}$ hours for 102 and O'Neill gained some revenge for first innings indignities by making 67, but they lost their ninth wicket early on the final morning at 334 and were 157 ahead when Davidson was joined by Graham McKenzie and decided to take the attack to the England bowlers and particularly David Allen, who had taken three wickets that morning.

Ken Barrington

66 Quite simply, we let their last wicket pair put on too many runs – 98 – so that what should have been a formality in our second innings turned into a sizeable target. During that stand Peter May, for some reason, just refused to take the new ball. We had it sewn up but then we fiddled about with the spinners. Then, as soon as we took the new ball, Flavell clean bowled Davidson! 99 **Fred Trueman**

Australia had made 432 and, what seemed more important, they had used up more valuable time, so that England now had only 230 minutes to score 256 runs.

66 That was quite a target for England, but it all looked plain sailing. Subba Row and Geoff Pullar went along quite easily, then Ted Dexter *(right)* came in and played another of his super innings for 76. He was playing absolutely magnificently. He was undoubtedly at his best against fast bowling – he could perhaps look a bit scary sometimes against the slows. He was upright and you didn't want to field at mid-on or mid-off when he was in full flow. 99 Brian Johnston

🎙 *REX ALSTON*
And its Mackay and an imperious stroke from Dexter, four runs to mid-wicket! Dexter moves to 69 and England move to 143 for 1 and that must have narrowed the gap between runs and minutes still more. Dexter's 13th four in 69 runs. Yes 113 runs wanted in 112 minutes. Mackay comes in again and Dexter has hit that high in the air and it is going to be six into the crowd, is it? It is. Dexter 75, England 149 for 1. Jack, this is entertainment deluxe.

JACK FINGLETON This is 100 per cent good, Rex, magnificent.
🎙 *REX ALSTON*
Yes. And now the run rate is under a run a minute, as Mackay bowls again to Dexter who plays that gently towards mid-wicket for a single and that is the 150 up, 76 to Dexter, 45 to Subba Row. The innings now has been in progress for two hours and one minute.

ENGLAND
SECOND INNINGS
150-1

Richie Benaud was now thrown on the defence. But he had one last ploy, which he discussed the previous evening with Ray Lindwall as they looked at the worn marks made by the faster bowlers' follow-through outside a right hander's leg stump at one end. Lindwall had advised

Benaud that he might use these footholds if the batsmen were on the attack as a defensive measure, though he would have to be very accurate. This now seemed to be the moment. Benaud switched to bowling round the wicket with immediate success. Dexter was caught behind for 76. Enter the England captain …

REX ALSTON

And it is Benaud to May. Now this is an intriguing duel as May pushes out and the ball goes behind the wicket on the leg side fielded by Burge. I notice that Benaud has still got his outfield with the one that he had for Dexter, I do not anticipate that May is going to lob one into the outfield quite yet, if he does at all. But he has had a go at that! Has he been bowled round his legs? Must have been. Bowled for 0, round his legs. He stood there and swung, and he has quite certainly bowled him. May could not believe it. And May is out bowled Benaud 0. What a funny game cricket is.

JACK FINGLETON

Well, what a transition now; much as we saw this morning when three Australian wickets fell in no time, for hardly any runs at all and then we had that magnificent last wicket partnership between Alan Davidson and Graham McKenzie. Now, just at a time when Dexter, with the magnificent support of Subba Row, had completely pulverised the Australian attack and England had it where they wanted it, May is bowled second ball and the game is taking another sudden twist. What a magnificent Test match this has been.

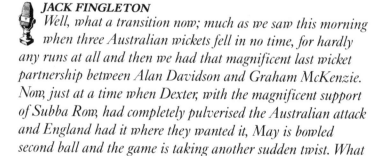

ENGLAND
SECOND INNINGS
150-3

66 It was about this point that Gubby Allen got into his Rolls Royce and was driving back to London, confident that England had the game in the bag.

Then Close went in and he was unbelievable. He went bananas. He gave it a tremendous wa-hoo and played across the line. It looked dreadful. If it had come off it would have been alright, but it didn't. He was caught round the corner, off Benaud (*far left*), and then came the collapse. It was absolutely incredible – from a certain win we had lost it. **99**

Brian Johnston

Benaud's triumph

66The embarrassment of losing so badly was too much. They had to have a scapegoat so they put the blame on me, saying that the footmarks I made with my follow-through gave Richie the chance to bowl us out. I was dropped for the next match and very hurt.99   **Fred Trueman**

66I suppose it was Fred Trueman who carved the pitch up, but you don't blame a man for that, really. If a bowler is as daring and accurate enough as Benaud was he deserves what he gets. Benaud always had one of the best cricketing brains.99   **John Arlott**

66This was Richie's day. Undoubtedly a great bowler and a marvellous, inspirational captain. However, he did start the awful kissing. I remember asking him about this and he said: "Well, I'll do anything as long as it encourages the players.99   **Brian Johnston**

Close had hit one six, but the rough into which Benaud was bowling was going to create problems for a left-hander like Close outside his off stump. The left-handed Subba Row had played the anchor role for Dexter's innings, then watched with dismay as three wickets fell for eight runs. However, just before tea Benaud yorked him for 49. England still believed they could win, but soon afterwards they were thrown onto defence by the loss of Barrington, lbw to a limping Ken Mackay. Now that England were thinking only of saving the game, Benaud had returned to bowling over the wicket, because from the previous angle, the batsmen were now prepared to play with their pads, which they could do with safety. He had Murray and Allen caught at slip by Simpson, who then had Trueman caught by Benaud. The last pair hung on for a while, but Davidson accounted for Statham and Australia had achieved a remarkable win by 54 runs and in doing so assured the retention of the Ashes.

Fourth Test, Old Trafford, 27 July-1 August 1961
Australia won by 54 runs

AUSTRALIA

W. M. Lawry lbw b Statham	74	c Trueman b Allen	102
R. B. Simpson c Murray b Statham	4	c Murray b Flavell	51
R. N. Harvey c Subba Row b Statham	19	c Murray b Dexter	35
N. C. O'Neill hit wkt b Trueman	11	c Murray b Statham	67
P. J. Burge b Flavell	15	c Murray b Dexter	23
B. C. Booth c Close b Statham	46	lbw b Dexter	9
K. D. Mackay c Murray b Statham	11	c Close b Allen	18
A. K. Davidson c Barrington b Dexter	0	not out	77
*R. Benaud b Dexter	2	lbw b Allen	1
†A. T. W. Grout c Murray b Dexter	2	c Statham b Allen	0
G. D. McKenzie not out	1	b Flavell	32
Extras (b4, lb1)	5	(b6, lb9, w2)	17
Total	**190**		**432**

ENGLAND

G. Pullar b Davidson	63	c O'Neill b Davidson	26
R. Subba Row c Simpson b Davidson	2	b Benaud	49
E. R. Dexter c Davidson b McKenzie	16	c Grout b Benaud	76
*P. B. H. May c Simpson b Davidson	95	b Benaud	0
D. B. Close lbw b McKenzie	33	c O'Neill b Benaud	8
K. F. Barrington c O'Neill b Simpson	78	lbw b Mackay	5
†J. T. Murray c Grout b Mackay	24	c Simpson b Benaud	4
D. A. Allen c Booth b Simpson	42	c Simpson b Benaud	10
F. S. Trueman c Harvey b Simpson	3	c Benaud b Simpson	8
J. B. Statham c Mackay b Simpson	4	b Davidson	8
J. A. Flavell not out	0	not out	0
Extras (b2, lb4, w1)	7	(b5, w2)	7
Total	**367**		**201**

ENGLAND	O	M	R	W		O	M	R	W
Trueman	14	1	55	1	–	32	6	92	0
Statham	21	3	53	5	–	44	9	106	1
Flavell	22	8	61	1	–	29.4	4	65	2
Dexter	6.4	2	16	3	–	20	4	61	3
Allen					–	38	25	58	4
Close					–	8	1	33	0
AUSTRALIA									
Davidson	39	11	70	3	–	14.4	1	50	2
McKenzie	38	11	106	2	–	4	1	20	0
Mackay	40	9	81	1	–	13	7	33	1
Benaud	35	15	80	0	–	32	11	70	6
Simpson	11.4	4	23	4	–	8	4	21	1

AUSTRALIA **fall of wickets**
FIRST INNINGS: 1-8, 2-51, 3-89, 4-106, 5-150, 6-174, 7-185, 8-185, 9-189.
SECOND INNINGS: 1-113, 2-175, 3-210, 4-274, 5-290, 6-296, 7-332, 8-334, 9-334.
ENGLAND **fall of wickets**
FIRST INNINGS: 1-3, 2-43, 3-154, 4-212, 5-212, 6-272, 7-358, 8-362, 9-367.
SECOND INNINGS: 1-40, 2-150, 3-150, 4-158, 5-163, 6-171, 7-171, 8, 189, 9-193.

First Test at Edgbaston, June 8-13
Match drawn
England 195 (Subba Row 59) and 401-4 (Dexter 180, Subba Row 112); Australia 516-9 dec (Harvey 114, O'Neill 82, Simpson 76, Mackay 64, Lawry 57).

Second Test at Lord's, June 22-26
Australia won by 5 wickets.
England 206 (Davidson 5-42) and 202 (Barrington 66, McKenzie 5-37); Australia 340 (Lawry 130, Mackay 54) and 71-5.

Third Test at Headingley, July 6-8
England won by 8 wickets
Australia 237 (Harvey 73, McDonald 54, Trueman 5-58) and 120 (Harvey 53, Trueman 6-30); England 299 (Cowdrey 93, Pullar 53, Davidson 5-63) and 62-2.

Fifth Test at The Oval, August 17-22
Match drawn
England 256 (May 71, Barrington 53) and 370-8 (Subba Row 137, Barrington 83, Mackay 5-121); Australia 494 (Burge 181, O'Neill 177, Booth 71).

AUSTRALIA IN ENGLAND 1964

The Fifth Test, **The Oval,** *August 13-18 1964*
Commentators **Rex Alston, John Arlott, Alan McGilvray,**
Robert Hudson
Summariser **Jack Fingleton**

This series was really decided by one innings. At Headingley, in the Third Test, after two rain-affected draws, Australia were reduced to 178 for 7 in reply to England's 268, with only Peter Burge of the recognised batsmen left.

❝If Burge had been out then, Australia would have been in a great deal of trouble. But he played an innings in which he was on top of everything. He was not the greatest of batsmen, though he was a very good one and on this occasion Fred Trueman and Jack Flavell bowled short at him and he hooked bravely and magnificently and, as far as I am concerned, it is the only instance of a single innings winning a Test rubber.❞
John Arlott

One that got away ... Burge, the hero of Leeds, is put down off Trueman.

His 160 certainly won that Test, by seven wickets, with more than a day to spare and the Australian captain, Bobby Simpson, knew now that he only needed one draw to retain the Ashes. He achieved this at Old Trafford off his own bat, making 311 in 13 hours in an Australian total of 656 for 8 declared. England's retaliatory weapon was Ken Barrington who made 256, aided by his captain Ted Dexter's 174 in a score of 611 to kill a game they had already been batted out of.

In the final Test at The Oval, Neil Hawke bundled England out soon after tea on the first day for 182.

Bill Lawry led the reply with a patient, unexciting 94, to follow his patient, unexciting, hundred at Old Trafford. Australia were in the lead on the second day, but the most memorable moment of the match was saved for Saturday.

Fred Trueman, the leading taker of Test wickets in the world, with 297, had been recalled to this match after missing Old Trafford. Could he take his tally to 300?

Bobby Simpson

 JOHN ARLOTT

Trueman with a bit of a scowl at the batsman. Doesn't even look friendly towards his fieldsmen at the moment. In his 31st over. Has 2 wickets. Wants a third. Trueman in again. Bowls to Hawke … and Hawke goes forward and is caught! There's the 300th! There was no nicer touch than Trueman congratulating Hawke. Caught by Cowdrey! Neil Hawke can never have come into the pavilion to a greater ovation in his life but they weren't looking at him. Fred Trueman's 300th Test wicket. The first man in the history of cricket to achieve the figure when Hawke played a half-hearted stroke outside the off stump to a ball that took the outside edge and Cowdrey swooped on it, 2 hands. It was high in the air, up went Trueman, up went the crowd, stood to him, cheered him, and as Hawke walked away Trueman congratulated him.

Fred Trueman

 ***JACK FINGLETON***

A nice neat catch by Cowdrey and my heartfelt congratulations, as an Australian, to one of the greatest fighters we've ever had against us. This chap is never beaten. He's put everything he's got into the game and it couldn't have happened to a greater fighter. Well done, Freddie Trueman.

AUSTRALIA
FIRST INNINGS
367-9

66 People had been expecting me to do it and things had gone quite well in the field – I had caught a couple of catches. But as we moved towards lunch on the third day, Australia had started to get on top. The spinners had been on too long, nobody really knew what to do, so I put myself on. I grabbed the ball and told Ted "I'll have a go, skipper". Almost immediately, I bowled Ian Redpath middle stump and, next ball, I had Graham McKenzie caught by Cowdrey. Then I had to suffer the longest forty minutes of my life because there was no time to continue the over. We all trooped off for lunch with me on a hat-trick, needing one wicket for the 300. I didn't have any lunch, I couldn't concentrate on anything. I was just dying to get back out in the middle.

Then finally, there I was facing Neil Hawke. I bowled but I just didn't bowl it straight. Who knows what might have happened if we hadn't had to stop for a lunch I didn't eat!

Then came the moment when I got Neil Hawke and took the 300th wicket. 99   **Fred Trueman**

66 It was an amusing moment, because to see Fred preen himself was quite amazing. He just didn't know what to do, whether to stand on his head, to jump over the moon or what. If ever a man was delirious with happiness it was Fred when he took that 300th wicket. 99   **John Arlott**

Trueman catches Tom Veivers (*above*) and Colin Cowdrey catches Neil Hawke to give Fred Trueman his 300th Test wicket (*right*)

72

❝Strangely, I didn't feel anything at all when it happened, probably, I think, because I felt there was still a wicket to get, and I did – Corling for nought.

It was only afterwards that I realised the impact it had had on the cricket world. There were telegrams from all over the place – except Yorkshire, of course. Up until that point I don't think anybody thought it would be possible to take 300 wickets in Test cricket. I was 34 at the time. I remember someone asking me if the achievement would ever be repeated. I said "Aye, but whoever does it will be bloody tired."❞

Fred Trueman

❝I thought, as many people did, that that was a record to last a lifetime, because I don't think anybody quite anticipated the plethora of Test Matches there is now.❞

John Arlott

❝The great thing about Fred is that not only did he take 307 Test wickets but look how many he took every year for Yorkshire! By comparison with his record for his county, what modern Test bowlers like Willis or Snow ever did was negligible.

I know he says that if he had been picked in more Tests he would have taken 400 wickets and he probably would have done.

He was one of these characters you could not take your eyes off while he was performing.

He was quick and had the ability to get close to the stumps with his marvellous swivel action and swing the ball away. Immensely strong. How often was he injured? Very rarely.❞

Brian Johnston

Australia had taken a first innings lead of 197, but another Yorkshireman's effort, in combination with a last day washed out, made sure that England saved the game.

JOHN ARLOTT

Well now, this man wants two for his hundred. Corling bowls and Boycott gets over it . . . doesn't time it properly, hits it quite hard and uninhibitedly into the covers. O'Neill fields. It'll be his first Test hundred, of course. Five men saving the one, two up for the catch. Corling comes in, bowls outside the off stump . . . there it is! Four runs right of cover's left hand. It crosses the ropes, beats Lawry. Boycott a hundred and two. Arthur Wrigley passes me a note to say a hundred in 3 hours 55 minutes with 9 fours, and I believe by no means the last Test hundred we'll see from this man.

❝There was never any doubt about Geoffrey Boycott's ability. He was, I suppose, the ultimate perfectionist. It positively hurt him in the heart, I think, to play a bad stroke, certainly if it got him out. I don't think he was dull, he was just so deadly efficient and the fact is that he made runs against good opposition, even the best opposition. He took it on and tackled it and made his runs. Geoffrey earned his runs the hard way. He wasn't the funniest man, he wasn't the most humorous of men and, whether you call him a perfectionist or a self-seeker, I don't think it matters. He was as near to the perfect batsman as I've seen.❞ **John Arlott**

Boycott's first Test century (above) followed a score of 30 in the first innings (right)

Fifth Test, The Oval, 13-18 August 1964
Match drawn

ENGLAND

G. Boycott b Hawke	30	c Redpath b Simpson	113	
R. W. Barber b Hawke	24	lbw b McKenzie	29	
*E. R. Dexter c Booth b Hawke	23	c Simpson b McKenzie	25	
M. C. Cowdrey c Grout b McKenzie	20	not out	93	
K. F. Barrington c Simpson b Hawke	47	not out	54	
P. H. Parfitt b McKenzie	3			
†J. M. Parks c Simpson b Corling	10			
F. J. Titmus c Grout b Hawke	8	b McKenzie	56	
F. S. Trueman c Redpath b Hawke	14			
T. W. Cartwright c Grout b McKenzie	0			
J. S. E. Price not out	0			
Extras (lb4)	3	(b6, lb4, nb1)	11	
Total	**182**	**(4 wkts)**	**381**	

AUSTRALIA

*R. B. Simpson c Dexter b Cartwright	24
W. M. Lawry c Trueman b Dexter	94
N. C. O'Neill c Parfitt b Cartwright	11
P. J. Burge lbw b Titmus	25
B. C. Booth c Trueman b Price	74
I. R. Redpath b Trueman	45
†A. W. T. Grout b Cartwright	20
T. R. Veivers not out	67
G. D. McKenzie c Cowdrey b Trueman	0
N. J. N. Hawke c Cowdrey b Trueman	14
G. E. Corling c Parfitt b Trueman	0
Extras (b4, lb1)	5
Total	**379**

BOWLING

AUSTRALIA	O	M	R	W		O	M	R	W
McKenzie	26	6	87	3	–	33	5	112	3
Corling	14	2	32	1	–	25	4	65	0
Hawke	25.4	8	47	6	–	39	8	89	0
Veivers	6	1	13	0	–	47	15	90	0
Simpson					–	14	7	14	1

ENGLAND	O	M	R	W	
Trueman	33.3	6	87	4	–
Price	21	2	67	1	–
Cartwright	62	23	110	3	–
Titmus	42	20	51	1	–
Barber	6	1	23	0	–
Dexter	13	1	36	1	–

ENGLAND fall of wickets
FIRST INNINGS: 1-44, 2-61, 3-82, 4-111, 5-117, 6-141, 7-160, 8-173, 9-174.
SECOND INNINGS: 1-80, 2-120, 3-200, 4-255.
AUSTRALIA fall of wickets
FIRST INNINGS: 1-45, 2-57, 3-96, 4-202, 5-245, 6-279, 7-343, 8-343, 9-367.

First Test at Trent Bridge, June 4-9
Match drawn
England 216-8 dec and 193-9 dec (Dexter 68, McKenzie 5-53); Australia 168 (Simpson 50) and 40-2.

Second Test at Lord's, June 18-23
Match drawn
Australia 176 (Veivers 54, Trueman 5-48) and 168-4 (Burge 59); England 246 (Edrich 120).

Third Test at Headingley, July 2-7
Australia won by 7 wickets
England 268 (Parks 68, Dexter 66, Hawke 5-75) and 229 (Barrington 85); Australia 389 (Burge 160, Lawry 78) and 111-3 (Redpath 58*).

Fourth Test at Old Trafford, July 23-28
Match drawn
Australia 656-8 dec (Simpson 311, Lawry 106, Booth 98) and 4-0; England 611 (Barrington 256, Dexter 174, Parks 60, Boycott 58, McKenzie 7-153).

AUSTRALIA IN ENGLAND 1968

The Fifth Test, **The Oval,** *August 22-27, 1968*
Commentators **John Arlott, Robert Hudson** *and* **Alan McGilvray**
Summarisers **Trevor Bailey, Norman Yardley** *and* **E. W. Swanton**

The fate of the Ashes has been already decided before the two sides assembled at The Oval for the final Test. By virtue of their victory in the First Test at Old Trafford by 159 runs, followed by three draws, all of which England had the better of, Australia had retained them again.

The most significant individual event, before The Oval, came in the Third Test at Edgbaston where Colin Cowdrey, in his 100th Test, made 104 not out. Somewhat improbably, Cowdrey had been given Geoff Boycott as a runner when he injured a leg during the innings – an injury which led to Tom Graveney taking over the captaincy for the Fourth Test. Cowdrey's sense-of-occasion hundred was his penultimate for England.

But the final Test is the match which sticks in the memory of all who saw it or listened to its dramatic climax on Test Match Special. That memory is preserved because of the feats of a young bowler, a batsman who played an innings that was to have political repercussions and the mopping up efforts of a crowd.

For the previous Test both captains had been absent with injuries, but now Cowdrey and Bill Lawry returned and it was Cowdrey who won the toss for England and elected to bat first on an easy paced Oval pitch. Colin Milburn went with the score at 28 before Lawry brought on his spinners, John Gleeson and Ashley Mallett, playing in his first Test match. At 84 Gleeson bowled Dexter for 21 and at 113 Cowdrey became Mallet's first Test victim, lbw for 16. But the England batting line-up was mightily impressive and the loss of Dexter and Cowdrey merely served to bring in Tom Graveney to join John Edrich. These two set about the building of a sound fourth wicket partnership.

Colin Cowdrey

ENGLAND
FIRST INNINGS
188-3

ALAN McGILVRAY
John Edrich is a man of great experience, but there is a little sign of nervousness and a little anxiety. Who would not be nervous at 99 in a Test match. Now Gleeson bowls, Edrich turns it away and there is a single there for him and it is his hundred. Edrich 100, score 3 for 188.

It is typical of John Edrich, particularly when he was batting against Australia, that he was not satisfied with just a hundred. He lost the company of Graveney, caught at slip off McKenzie for 63, after a stand of 125. But, by the close of the first day, another major partnership had started to build, as Edrich was joined by the late inclusion to the side, Basil D'Oliveira. It was 272 for 4 that night, but the fifth wicket continued to grow next day in its blend of styles – doggedness from Edrich and flamboyance from D'Oliveira until they had put on 121, at which point Edrich was bowled by Ian Chappell for 164. Alan Knott stayed with D'Oliveira to bring up the 400 and D'Oliveira's hundred. It was a great moment, not just for the man himself, but for Graveney, his Worcestershire captain, who had assured Cowdrey that he was in the right form for this match.

66I liked Basil very much indeed; I helped, I think, to get him over to this country and into first-class cricket here and I found that a most exciting and satisfying innings and so, I'm sure, did he.**99**
John Arlott

Basil D'Oliveira

77

Knott was caught behind off Mallett for 28 after they had put on 62 and now it was D'Oliveira who reached his 150 with eight wickets down and was last out for 158.

Australia started their first innings facing a total of 494 with 90 minutes of the second day to go. Milburn picked Inverarity up superbly at short leg for 1, but the second wicket pair were the intractable Lawry and Redpath, who frustrated the England bowlers until after lunch on Saturday, adding 129 before Redpath was caught at slip off Snow for 67. It had been a good enough start but now David Brown and Ray Illingworth reduced them to 188 for 6, still some way from saving the follow on. Lawry now found support from Graham McKenzie ...

ALAN McGILVRAY

Lawry 99; McKenzie 8; 6 for 217. Last ball, I think, of the over for Lawry to face Illingworth and it's turned on the on side and there is his hundred! A beautiful shot past mid-wicket and it is a well played solid innings. Lawry 103, 6 for 221 and he receives congratulations from McKenzie and great applause from this big crowd here today. I think they valued his innings in the context that he played it. A solid, hard innings, he has reached 103, 221 for 6.

**AUSTRALIA
FIRST INNINGS
221-6**

Lawry was out first thing on Monday morning, caught at the wicket off Snow for his week-end score of 135, and Australia were 269 for 8. They were indebted to Mallett for avoiding the follow-on, the debutant scoring 43 not out and with Gleeson, who made 19, the last Australian wicket fell at 324.

With a day and a half to go, England needed quick runs to add to their lead of 170. Only Cowdrey, who top scored with 35, stayed in more than an hour, and in three hours they scored 181 all out, which left Australia a target of 352 with 35 minutes of the fourth day to go. England took two wickets, Lawry departing to another Milburn short leg catch for 4 and Derek Underwood having Redpath lbw for 8. Australia were 13 for 2.

If Australians were praying for rain, their pleas went unanswered as the final day, like the four before it, dawned bright and sunny. The only cloud on their horizon was Underwood on a pitch that was beginning to turn ...

JOHN ARLOTT
Chappell going out, critically prodding a spot there outside his off stump. He settles, Underwood comes in, bowls, and Chappell covers up and he is lbw! That one nipped through and Chappell is lbw bowled Underwood 2 and Australia are 19 for 3.

ROBERT HUDSON
So it is Underwood meanwhile from the Vauxhall end up to Walters … My goodness, he is caught at the wicket off the outside edge! It rose and left him and Knott took the catch, Walters is out, caught Knott bowled Underwood for 1 and Australia are 29 for 4. A very nasty one that lifted and turned.
Paul Sheahan, whose cover fielding had been one of the highlights of the series, stayed with Inverarity and made 24, before Illingworth had him – fifth out at 65. Although 20 more were added by Inverarity and Jarman before lunch, nothing, it seemed, could save Australia now.

A small army, armed with brooms, blankets, buckets and forks, soaked up, swept off or spiked away the water.

Mid-way through the lunch interval it appeared that the visitors had conjured up some old aboriginal rain dance. Abruptly and violently a thunderstorm broke over Kennington and in no time the ground was awash and, as if to mock England, within an hour of the storm's start the sun was shining brightly on puddles that resembled lakes. No one believed that there could be a chance of any further play. From the Australian dressing room came the sounds of celebration, but Cowdrey had other ideas. He encouraged groundstaff and members of the crowd to join in an extraordinary mopping-up operation.

The mopping up had taken just two-and-a-half hours when play was eventually possible, but it left only 75 minutes for England to try to capture the last five wickets. For half an hour opener Inverarity and wicketkeeper Jarman remained defiant ...

AUSTRALIA
SECOND INNINGS
105-5

ROBERT HUDSON
Underwood goes briskly back, anxious to get in as much bowling as possible. There are just 45 minutes left to play. Five wickets to get, Underwood up, bowls and this again is swung round by Inverarity from his leg stump, down on the leg side for four more runs and that is his 50. A very courageous 50 indeed, applauded by the whole of the England side and, as they are all gathered round him in a ring, he gets the full force of their applause!

TREVOR BAILEY
And he is seldom going to play a better innings for Australia. In terms of value to his side, this is a very, very fine performance by a young, comparatively inexperienced player who has adapted his game to these conditions which are entirely foreign to him. Now England have made yet another bowling change introducing D'Oliveira who will presumably bowl off cutters, his added pace may prove effective.

Up to now the pitch had been too wet for Underwood to get any purchase, but this was a crucial change ...

AUSTRALIA
SECOND INNINGS
110-6

ROBERT HUDSON
It is minutes that count now, 36 minutes to get five wickets is a very tall order indeed and England's hopes must be dwindling rapidly. D'Oliveira comes up, bowls, this is outside the off stump ... Oh he has bowled him! He has bowled him, good gracious! He just nipped the off bail when Jarman padded up and I thought the ball had gone through, it must have just nipped off the off bail ...
So it is the phlegmatic Mallett. Has a good look round the field — did not have far to look — settles in and Underwood comes in and he is caught! He is caught at short leg by Brown, Mallett is out. That ball popped; Brown took the catch, literally, off the bat. The second short leg from the left I suppose you would describe that and at last Underwood got one to pop and the close in fielders got the catch they had been striving for so long. So it is 110 for 7.

AUSTRALIA
SECOND INNINGS
110-7

ALAN McGILVRAY
It is Underwood now to bowl to McKenzie, McKenzie
forward and hits the inside of the bat and skids up on to
the chest of Knott. Now that is a fairly ominous sign for the
Australians. The wicket now, as Trevor indicated, taking a
little bit of bite. It is very difficult to place these fieldsmen. Let
us say there is a complete ring of nine fieldsmen around the bat
from fine leg down to fly slip and back comes Underwood,
bowls to McKenzie, McKenzie forward and it is another lovely
catch! This is a good catch by Brown, yes he caught that and

caught it well, that was low down, took it almost off the
ground, he quickly picked it up and ran back to the umpire
appealing. No need to because McKenzie walked but the catch
was well made, just moving forward, he took it inches from the
ground, going in underneath it, he made a splendid catch of
that to dismiss McKenzie who also failed to score. Now the
Australians are in dire trouble with but Gleeson and Connolly
to follow and 27 minutes to play …
So, 12 minutes to go, now Underwood decides to bowl left arm
round the wicket and umpire Elliott indicated to Gleeson that
he is coming in from that side and Underwood goes in now to
bowl to Gleeson and Gleeson forward and he's bowled him! He
let it go and he clean bowled him. He made no attempt to play
it; it was dead on line all the way; he left his bat on his
shoulder and he found his off stump on the ground and so
Australia are 9 wickets down for 120. Gleeson bowled by
Underwood for 5, Australia 9 for 120 and 11 minutes to play.

AUSTRALIA
SECOND INNINGS
110-8

AUSTRALIA
SECOND INNINGS
120-9

JOHN ARLOTT

Underwood hammering away, bustling back to his mark, tossing the ball from hand to hand, nervous strain on both sides now. A situation in which a bowler could press too much. Underwood comes in, bowls and he has padded away and he is out! Played deliberately with his pad, Inverarity. Just missed carrying his bat to a ball that just about

66On wet wickets he was a great destroyer, like most finger spinners, but the fact is that he could bowl, as he showed often in over-limit games, defensively on a good wicket and very skilfully. He could control his length and line. He didn't give it the flight of many slow bowlers, of course. He didn't toss it up; he didn't invite the drive, but he was a most precise and accurate bowler. If he was a killer on a turning wicket, he was also a bit of a master of defence on a good one.**99**   **John Arlott**

straightened. Inverarity is lbw bowled Underwood and any moment now Bill Frindall will tell me how many England have won by, they have won by 226. Australia retain the Ashes but England have tied the series and perhaps made good some of their disappointments from the Tests at Lord's and Edgbaston, and the smallest but the happiest crowd of the match standing in front of the pavilion cheering.

Derek Underwood had finished with the fine figures of 7 for 50 from 31 overs and three balls.

There is an unhappy postscript to this match. Basil D'Oliveira, the man whose innings launched England toward victory and who started the final Australian slide with the wicket of Jarman, was not included in the MCC party announced shortly afterwards for the winter tour of South Africa. Not long after that announcement, though, he was included, after all, when Tom Cartwright had to withdraw. But the media attention surrounding the late inclusion of a Cape Coloured was too much for the South African government, who refused to accept D'Oliveira. England have not played South Africa since.

AUSTRALIA
SECOND INNINGS
125 all out

Fifth Test, The Oval, 22-27 August 1968
England won by 226 runs

ENGLAND

J. H. Edrich b Chappell	164	c Lawry b Mallett	17
C. Milburn b Connolly	8	c Lawry b Connolly	18
E. R. Dexter b Gleeson	21	b Connolly	28
*M. C. Cowdrey lbw b Mallett	16	b Mallett	35
T. W. Graveney c Redpath b McKenzie	63	run out	12
B. L. D'Oliveira c Inverarity b Mallett	158	c Gleeson b Connolly	9
†A. P. Knott c Jarman b Mallett	28	run out	34
R. Illingworth lbw b Connolly	8	b Gleeson	10
J. A. Snow run out	4	c Sheahan b Gleeson	13
D. L. Underwood not out	9	not out	1
D. J. Brown c Sheahan b Gleeson	2	b Connolly	1
Extras (b1, lb11, w1)	13	(lb3)	3
Total	**494**		**181**

AUSTRALIA

*W. M. Lawry c Knott b Snow	135	c Milburn b Brown	4
R. J. Inverarity c Milburn b Snow	1	lbw b Underwood	56
I. R. Redpath c Cowdrey b Snow	67	lbw b Underwood	8
I. M. Chappell c Knott b Brown	10	lbw b Underwood	2
K. D. Walters c Knott b Brown	5	c Knott b Underwood	1
A. P. Sheahan b Illingworth	14	c Snow b Illingworth	24
†B. N. Jarman st Knott b Illingworth	0	b D'Oliveira	21
G. D. McKenzie b Brown	12	c Brown b Underwood	0
A. A. Mallett not out	43	c Brown b Underwood	0
J. W. Gleeson c Dexter b Underwood	19	b Underwood	5
A. N. Connolly b Underwood	3	not out	0
Extras (b4, lb7, nb4)	15	(lb4)	4
Total	**324**		**125**

BOWLING

AUSTRALIA	O	M	R	W		O	M	R	W
McKenzie	40	8	87	1	–	4	0	14	0
Connolly	57	12	127	2	–	22.4	2	65	4
Walters	6	2	17	0	–				
Gleeson	41.2	8	109	2	–	7	2	22	2
Mallett	36	11	87	3	–	25	4	77	2
Chappell	21	5	54	1					
ENGLAND									
Snow	35	12	67	3	–	11	5	22	0
Brown	22	5	63	3	–	8	3	19	1
Illingworth	48	15	87	2	–	28	18	29	1
Underwood	54.3	21	89	2	–	31.3	19	50	7
D'Oliveira	4	2	3	0	–	5	4	1	1

ENGLAND fall of wickets
FIRST INNINGS: 1-28, 2-84, 3-113, 4-238, 5-359, 6-421, 7-458, 8-468, 9-489.
SECOND INNINGS: 1-23, 2-53, 3-67, 4-90, 5-114, 6-126, 7-149, 8-179, 9-179.
AUSTRALIA fall of wickets
FIRST INNINGS: 1-7, 2-136, 3-151, 4-161, 5-185, 6-188, 7-237, 8-269, 9-302.
SECOND INNINGS: 1-4, 2-13, 3-19, 4-29, 5-65, 6-110, 7-110, 8-110, 9-120.

First Test at Old Trafford, June 6-11
Australia won by 159 runs
Australia 357 (Sheahan 88, Lawry 81, Walters 81, I. Chappell 73) and 220 (Walters 86, Pocock 6-79); England 165 and 253 (D'Oliveira 87*).

Second Test at Lord's, June 20-25
Match drawn
England 351-7 dec (Milburn 83, Barrington 75); Australia 78 (Brown 5-42) and 127-4 (Redpath 53).

Third Test at Edgbaston, July 11-16
Match drawn
England 409 (Cowdrey 104, Graveney 96, Edrich 88) and 142-3 dec (Edrich 64); Australia 222 (I. Chappell 71, Cowper 57) and 68-1.

Fourth Test at Headingley, July 25-30
Match drawn
Australia 315 (Redpath 92, I. Chappell 65) and 312 (I. Chappell 81, Walters 56, Illingworth 6-87); England 302 (Prideaux 64, Edrich 62, Connolly 5-72) and 230-4 (Edrich 65).

83

ENGLAND IN AUSTRALIA 1970/71

The Seventh Test, **Sydney,** *February 12-17, 1971*
Commentators **Brian Johnston, Alan McGilvray and Jim Burke**
Summariser **Lindsay Hassett**

Even by modern standards of overkill in international cricket, a seventh Test does sound somewhat extravagant. An extra Test match, though, had been added to the agreed itinerary as a result of the Third Test in Melbourne over the New Year being totally washed out. Australian determination to fit in the match must have gained impetus, too, following England's win a week later in Sydney which had given the tourists a one-nil lead in the series after two earlier draws. The England management's ready acceptance of their proposal had been one of several bones of contention between the captain, Ray Illingworth, and manager David Clark.

66It was unfortunate really because they had the wrong manager. They chose David Clark because they assumed that Colin Cowdrey was going to be captain and they were great friends. In those days they chose the manager first, the captain second. Then, of course, Cowdrey wasn't made captain and Illingworth (*right*) was chosen.

David was a very nice chap, but of course a complete opposite to Illy and things that Illy did would aggravate him terribly. Illy was much like Len Hutton. He was a captain that a team would work for, and he got the best of Boycott.

Furthermore he was quite tough. He got the best out of John Snow who gave the impression on that tour that he didn't try overmuch although he has always said he was injured. Certainly Snow hadn't done an awful lot up until Brisbane and Illy told me that he said to Snow: "Well, if you don't buck up, I'll send you home." He meant it and Snow got the message.99

MCC arrive at Adelaide

Snow and Boycott had played the leading roles in that win in that Fourth Test in Sydney. Boycott with 77 and 142 not out and Snow with 7 for 40 in the second innings. But now, instead of the original two, there were three Tests remaining for England to hold onto that lead and reclaim the Ashes which had been the property of the "enemy" for twelve years.

In the extra Test at Melbourne – officially the fifth – a large Australian total was answered with centuries from Brian Luckhurst and Basil D'Oliveira and the match was drawn. England had the upper hand in Adelaide, where Illingworth declined to enforce the follow-on to save his tiring pace bowlers. Geoff Boycott and John Edrich opened with a hundred partnership in each innings, Edrich making a century in the first and Boycott in the second. The match was drawn, thanks to Keith Stackpole and Ian Chappell each making a hundred in the second innings.

So they returned to Sydney with England still one up, but knowing that an Australian win would deny them the Ashes for at least another eighteen months. In their attempt to achieve that win, the Australian selectors made a change of captaincy, bringing in the pugnacious Ian Chappell to replace the stoical Bill Lawry. The groundsman, too, had done his bit to ensure a result and this Sydney pitch had already produced the only positive outcome of the series. When England had been put in and shot out for 184 on the first day, it seemed certain that it would do so again, even without the sixth day that had been allocated.

John Edrich

85

AUSTRALIA
FIRST INNINGS
11-1

Alan Knott

JIM BURKE
So Australia, no wicket for 11 in reply to the England first innings total of 184. Eastwood is 5 and Stackpole 6. Eastwood's runs have come from two pretty nice shots, turning the ball off his toes, whereas Stackpole's runs have come from a mishit over slips and a cut shot that wasn't truly well timed. Lever to Eastwood and he's caught is he? Yes, Eastwood is caught behind! Eastwood caught Knott bowled Lever for 5 and Australia 1 for 11.

LINDSAY HASSETT
Well, Knott made the catch look easy but it was quite a wide one. This was on, of course, with Lever bowling these big cartwheeling inswingers to the lefthander Eastwood. We saw him several times attempt the leg glance, very tempting too, because Illingworth had placed a leg slip, a backward square leg and a silly mid on, but no one at all down at fine leg on the fence. So Eastwood, going for the glance, was deceived by the fact that the ball just swung too much for him. He tried to play against it instead of hitting the ball in the centre of the bat, and got an inside edge. It diverted quite a lot and this, with the addition of the swing from Lever, did push the ball a long way wide of Knott down on the on side. But Knott moved across, I would say, some 2, 3, 4 yards and finished up taking the ball quite cleanly on the right hand side of his body. A very good catch from Knott but this is what we've come to expect from the English wicketkeeper. He certainly is right up in world class.

JIM BURKE
So, our clock showing about six minutes of play remaining this evening and we will assume that there will be one more over after this one from Snow. We have four slips standing in a most unusual formation, a straight line right across the ground with the gully fieldsman standing a good three yards in front of them. Fletcher is at first slip, D'Oliveira at second, Willis at third and Illingworth at fourth, Edrich in the gully and Luckhurst in the covers. So one ball remaining in this third over of Snow's. He comes in from the far end, bowls to Stackpole who ... is he caught? Yeah, no, bowled! Stackpole bowled Snow. Stackpole is out bowled Snow for 6 and Australia are 2 for 13.

AUSTRALIA
FIRST INNINGS
13-2

LINDSAY HASSETT
*Well, we anticipated some trouble for Australia, especially
if Snow really got some encouragement. I don't blame
Stackpole for being bowled although we can say technically he
left the gap in between bat and pad and the ball came back.
But, earlier in this over, Snow bowled about three or four
deliveries pitched on a good length or just short of a length
outside the off stump and the ball definitely cut away towards
the slips. And I noticed after the third one Stackpole walked up
the wicket to see where the ball was landing because this really
did spell some danger for him. It only needed a ball landing a
little bit closer to the line of the stumps somewhere roundabout
middle stump or middle and off stump and these, all of these
previous three deliveries would have been really dangerous,
because the ball cut away quickly towards the slips.*

*Now I think Stackpole with his last delivery moved over
to try and cover up this danger with the ball going away
towards the slips. He moved too far with his bat, didn't have
his pad quite close enough and the ball came back. It really was
a beautiful ball, came back beautifully from outside the off
stump and just tipped the outside of the off stump, enough to
remove the bail. The bail just fell to the ground. It wasn't
knocked back at all.*

This was just the start England needed and, the following
day, Peter Lever added the wicket of the nightwatchman,
Rod Marsh, Willis bowled the new captain, Ian Chappell,
for 25 and Australia were 66 for 4. Australia could have
done with the obdurate Lawry now, but they had the next
best thing in Ian Redpath who was joined by Doug
Walters in a stand of 81 for the fifth wicket. Redpath made
59 and Walters was favoured by being dropped three
times in his innings of 42. By the time Underwood
separated them, Australia were only 37 runs behind. Greg
Chappell, who, like Marsh and Lillee, started his Test
career in this series, took his side into the lead in a stay of
three hours, making 65.

Australia were already 51 ahead when the eighth
wicket fell and Terry Jenner came in to face a hostile John
Snow anxious to restrict the lead. What followed gave the
early morning listeners a rude awakening ...

Ian Chappell

87

BRIAN JOHNSTON

A few moments ago, Snow bowled a short ball which hit Jenner on the head. It knocked him down, he was taken off to tremendous boos and the result was that another batsman came in. Snow finished the over. Some words passed between him and umpire Lou Rowan. Lou Rowan said something to the other umpire. It could have been a warning for bumpers. It could have been something which Snow said.

Snow then came down to the hill below us here. Beer cans were thrown, not necessarily at him but they were thrown in the area where he was fielding, and Illingworth then called him up but Snow came back down here. Someone shook him by the hand in the crowd and patted him on the back but then there was another hail of cans thrown at him. They're also being thrown at the far end of the hill. The groundsman Athol Watkins is going out to collect some of them and when Snow came down here they bombarded him with cans. Illingworth came down with half his team, said something to Snow and he's led them off the field. It's an unprecedented position, this.

LINDSAY HASSETT

Yes, well I would have hoped that this type of thing would never have happened in Australia. I don't know where the blame really lies. First of all it lies with the crowd because this is very unruly behaviour and should never have taken place.

BRIAN JOHNSTON

There's about 50 minutes due for play. The two umpires are coming back on to the ground. There's something like about 20 policemen going around the outside trying to get rid of the cans from the field. There's about, I suppose, another 20 or 30 or 40 spectators on the ground, some of whom appear to be trying to get rid of the cans. And out comes the England side again being led by Ray Illingworth. You can listen to their reception. (Boos and jeers mingled with applause). The batsmen, by the way, never left the middle. And the police are now standing inside the ground to stop, I suppose, any more beer cans hitting anybody on the field. At the moment no more are being thrown. Those on the ground have been picked up by police and have been taken away. Willis has been sent down to field in the position where Snow was, underneath the little hill.

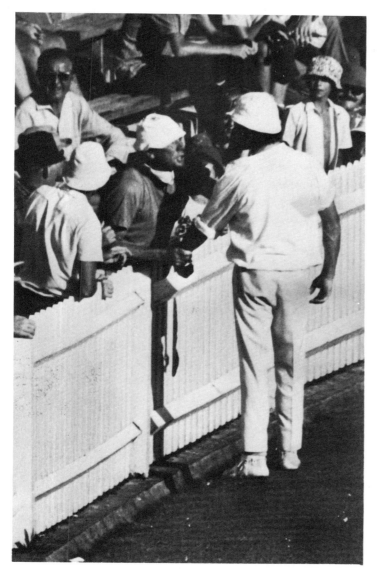

66 It was a case of whether John Snow should have been sent down to field at long leg after there had been a disturbance following the bouncer he bowled at Jenner. People have said that Illingworth shouldn't have sent him down there. But you should not have to be ruled by the crowd when it comes to where you place your field. I was watching very closely. They were booing and clapping, and a chap lent over and held his hand out to Snow. Snowy went to shake it and, as he did, another chap grabbed him by the shirt and that was the signal for a shower of bottles and cans.

Illy came down to see what was happening and Bob Willis arrived and made a few stupid gestures to the crowd. But basically Illy saw what was happening and took the team off. The interesting thing was that the umpires stayed in the middle. They never left the square to find out what was going on. The batsmen didn't move either.

So Illy led them off and the two umpires then went in and read the Riot Act to Illy and said: "Look, if you refuse to play we shall have to call the match off and award it to Australia."

Illy said: "Well, I'll play if the mess is cleared up. I'm not going out there if people are going to be bombarded. **99** **Brian Johnston**

Thereafter the crowd had an Australian lead of 80 to cheer and Jenner, who, incidentally, was no mean batsman, was last out for 30. On a pitch helpful to spinners and not unfriendly to any bowler, it was a handy lead, so the opening partnership between Edrich and Luckhurst, who had replaced the injured Boycott, which wiped out the deficit, was everything that Illingworth could have ordered. O'Keeffe got both men out in the fifties, but by that time England were 50 runs in the lead. There were

66 For England, I thought he was a marvellous bowler. He wasn't absolutely express but he had this lovely, slow, easy, loping run-up and he could be very very accurate. He swung the ball, moved it a little bit and had good line and length. And he could produce one or two very fast deliveries. He was quite hostile and he could be very unpleasant to play, but I wouldn't put him in the top league of quick bowlers. Again, he was an awkward character, a bit of a sulker, but if you got him in the right mood and got his pecker up he was a great bowler. He did very well on that tour. 99

Brian Johnston

John Snow (*above*) with broken hand and (*right*) bowling.

useful, if not obviously match-winning contributions all down the order after that, with D'Oliveira leading the rest with 47. Australia were eventually set 223 to win on the fourth day, with time no object. England needed a good start and Snow obliged in the first over, bowling Ken Eastwood, who had come in to replace Lawry in this, his only Test. Australia were 0 for 1. Immediately after striking this blow, though, Snow had another unhappy encounter on the boundary fence, this time with the fence itself, on which he broke his hand, attempting to catch a skier. The loss of England's most potent force seemed likely to be crucial.

Without Snow, Lever and Willis were still a useful attack. They accounted for Ian Chappell and Doug Walters cheaply, while Underwood removed Redpath and when the captain himself early next day bowled the dangerous Stackpole for 67, half the side had gone for 96. The possibility of the Ashes returning to England after such a time had put Test Match Special on the air just after midnight for the fifth day's play ...

BRIAN JOHNSTON
Waiting while Underwood adjusts his field. He's going over the wicket for the left-handed Marsh, bowling from the Randwick End, that's where the Hill is at the far end of the ground and it's Underwood coming in now over the wicket to bowl to Marsh. And that's clean bowled him! Marsh went for a big hit over mid-on. His leg stump is knocked out of the ground and Marsh is out. Underwood's got his wicket and Australia now 6 for 131 and I suppose Marsh will be regretting that stroke for an awful long time.

AUSTRALIA
SECOND INNINGS
131-6

LINDSAY HASSETT
Now well, of course, the odds are very much in favour of England. Very shortly Greg Chappell will have to think about trying to take control of this match and risking a lot to try and get quick runs because I don't believe that Australia, after the very bad start, will get out of this game through defensive means. They'll have to attack somewhere.

BRIAN JOHNSTON
Sixty-nine runs still needed and three wickets in hand. It's anybody's game at the moment. O'Keeffe is 12. Jenner 1. O'Keeffe facing up to D'Oliveira he turns this one down ... and he's caught! Caught there at square leg trying to hit outside the leg stump and it went straight into the hands of Shuttleworth who's fielding there as substitute for John Snow. So Shuttleworth gets his name in the book anyhow, as sub, and Australia have lost the valuable wicket of O'Keeffe. So O'Keeffe out and now applause as Lillee comes in. 154 eight wickets down. So again, the game swings back to England.

Right, now, we've got the first ball for Lillee ... and he's caught at second slip! First ball! He's appealing. He's looking round to Lou Rowan who gives him out. Lillee hesitating there. Now he touches his right pad. It went straight, it appeared, off the bat to Hampshire and Hampshire took the catch at second slip but Lillee paused for a moment there. One was not quite sure why. So this is really a little bit of a sensation. We now have one wicket to fall and a possible hat-trick. Now, whether the Ashes have ever been won on a hat-trick I wouldn't like to say but it is 154 for 9.

D'Oliveira was denied that personal milestone. However, shortly afterwards ...

AUSTRALIA
SECOND INNINGS
154-9

Derek Underwood

BRIAN JOHNSTON

Sixty-three runs still needed, one wicket to fall. So it's Underwood to bowl round the wicket to Jenner without a slip. A little bit strange that, but Jenner can have a good hit down to mid-wicket if he wants. Edrich is about half way back there. No-one deep down. Right, so, here is Underwood coming in, round the wicket from the Paddington end.

Bowls this very wide of the crease, a quicker one and it goes off bat and pad and he's caught! He's out caught! Underwood has got the wicket! Jenner's caught there by Fletcher at silly point and England have won the Ashes. England have won the Ashes back after 12 years and Illingworth is being chaired off by his team.

And, after commentating on England's triumph, Brian sat down to write the song of the Ashes.

We brought the Ashes back home.
We've got them here in the urn.
The Aussies had had them twelve years,
So it was about our turn.
But oh! What a tough fight
Its been in the dazzling sunlight.
In spite of the boos of the mob on the Hill,
We've won by two matches to nil.

❝Dreadful. To an old music hall tune called "Show me your winkle tonight", we put down the words to a song which the players thought would be the sort of hit that the England World Cup footballers had had. Vic Lewis conducted them — he'd got all the best session musicians and they gave their services free — and they thought this was a marvellous song. They all sang it and we recorded it in the Decca studios and made royalties of £53.86 pence. We decided it wasn't worth distributing so we put all the names in the hat and pulled out to see who would get the fabulous prize. I asked Illy to do the draw at the Test trial at Hove in '73. He drew his own name out of course.

They had a reception at Number 10 with Ted Heath. I sent him a copy of the music and I got a letter from him congratulating me on my "music and literary skills"! Always a politician!❞

Brian Johnston

Seventh Test, Sydney, 12-17 February 1971
England won by 62 runs

ENGLAND

J. H. Edrich c G. Chappell b Dell	30	c I. Chappell b O'Keeffe	57	
B. W. Luckhurst c Redpath b Walters	0	c Lillee b O'Keeffe	59	
K. W. R. Fletcher c Stackpole b O'Keeffe	33	c Stackpole b Eastwood	20	
J. H. Hampshire c Marsh b Lillee	10	c I. Chappell b O'Keeffe	24	
B. L. D'Oliveira b Dell	1	c I. Chappell b Lillee	47	
*R. Illingworth b Jenner	42	lbw b Lillee	29	
†A. P. Knott c Stackpole b O'Keeffe	27	b Dell	15	
J. A. Snow b Jenner	7	c Stackpole b Dell	20	
P. Lever c Jenner b O'Keeffe	4	c Redpath b Jenner	17	
D. L. Underwood not out	8	c Marsh b Dell	0	
R. G. D. Willis b Jenner	11	not out	2	
Extras (b4, lb4, w1, nb2)	11	(b3, lb3, nb6)	12	
Total	**184**		**302**	

AUSTRALIA

K. Eastwood c Knott b Lever	5	b Snow	0
K. R. Stackpole b Snow	6	b Illingworth	67
†R. W. Marsh c Willis b Lever	4	b Underwood	16
*I. M. Chappell b Willis	25	c Knott b Lever	6
I. R. Redpath c & b Underwood	59	c Hampshire b Illingworth	14
K. D. Walters st Knott b Underwood	42	c D'Oliveira b Willis	1
G. S. Chappell b Willis	65	st Knott b Illingworth	30
K. O'Keeffe c Knott b Illingworth	3	c sub b D'Oliveira	12
D. Lillee c Knott b Willis	6	c Hampshire b D'Oliveira	0
T. J. Jenner b Lever	30	c Fletcher b Underwood	4
A. Dell not out	3	not out	3
Extras (lb5, w1, nb10)	16	(b2, nb5)	7
Total	**264**		**160**

BOWLING

AUSTRALIA	O	M	R	W		O	M	R	W
Lillee	13	5	32	1	–	14	0	43	2
Dell	16	8	32	2	–	26.7	3	65	3
Walters	4	0	10	1	–	5	0	18	0
G. Chappell	3	0	9	0					
Jenner	16	3	42	3	–	21	5	39	1
O'Keeffe	24	8	48	3	–	26	8	96	3
Eastwood						5	0	21	1
Stackpole						3	1	8	0
ENGLAND									
Snow	18	2	68	1	–	2	1	7	1
Lever	14.6	3	43	3	–	12	2	23	1
D'Oliveira	12	3	24	0	–	5	1	15	2
Willis	12	1	58	3	–	9	1	32	1
Underwood	16	3	39	2	–	13.6	5	28	2
Illingworth	11	3	16	1	–	20	7	39	3
Fletcher						1	0	9	0

ENGLAND fall of wickets
FIRST INNINGS: 1-5, 2-60, 3-68, 4-69, 5-98, 6-145, 7-156, 8-165, 9-165.
SECOND INNINGS: 1-94, 2-125, 3-158, 4-165, 5-234, 6-251, 7-276, 8-298, 9-299.
AUSTRALIA fall of wickets
FIRST INNINGS: 1-11, 2-13, 3-32, 4-66, 5-147, 6-162, 7-178, 8-235, 9-239.
SECOND INNINGS: 1-0, 2-22, 3-71, 4-82, 5-96, 6-131, 7-142, 8-154, 9-154.

First Test at Brisbane, November 27-December 2
Match drawn
Australia 433 (Stackpole 207, Walters 112, I. Chappell 59, Snow 6-114) and 214 (Lawry 84, Shuttleworth 5-47); England 464 (Luckhurst 74, Edrich 79, Knott 73, D'Oliveira 57) and 39-1.

Second Test at Perth, December 11-16
Match drawn
England 397 (Luckhurst 131, Boycott 70) and 287-6 dec (Edrich 115*, Boycott 50); Australia 440 (Redpath 171, G. Chappell 108, I. Chappell 50) and 100-3.

Fourth Test at Sydney, January 9-14
England won by 299 runs
England 332 (Boycott 77, Edrich 55) and 319-5 dec (Boycott 142*, D'Oliveira 56, Illingworth 53); Australia 236 (Redpath 64, Walters 55) and 116 (Lawry 60*, Snow 7-40).

Fifth Test at Melbourne, January 21-26
Match drawn
Australia 493-9 dec (I. Chappell 111, Marsh 92*, Redpath 72, Lawry 56, Walters 55) and 169-4 dec; England 392 (D'Oliveira 117, Luckhurst 109) 161-0 (Boycott 76*, Edrich 74*).

Sixth Test at Adelaide, January 29-February 3
Match drawn
England 470 (Edrich 130, Fletcher 80, Boycott 58, Hampshire 55, Lillee 5-84) and 233-4 dec (Boycott 119*); Australia 235 (Stackpole 87) and 328-3 (Stackpole 136*, I. Chappell 104).

93

AUSTRALIA IN ENGLAND 1972

The Second Test, **Lord's,** *June 22-26*
Commentators **John Arlott, Brian Johnston and Alan McGilvray**
Summarisers **Trevor Bailey and Alan Davidson**

The Lord's Test of 1972 will always be remembered as Massie's match. Bob Massie, a 25-year-old medium pace swing bowler from Western Australia, was to stride across the international cricket stage in a brief, but glorious moment of limelight.

Massie had missed the first Test at Old Trafford which England had won, with the not inconsiderable help of a new cap, Tony Greig. But, for Lord's, the torn rib muscles which had kept him out in Manchester had mended and, when he looked out of his hotel window on the morning of his Test debut, Massie saw grey skies and considered the weather perfect. The skies were so grey that the two captains, Ray Illingworth of England and Ian Chappell of Australia, were turned back on the pavilion steps, by a short shower which delayed the start by half an hour. In the conditions, but with an outfield now damp enough to wet the ball, it was a difficult decision for Illingworth when he won the toss. He decided to bat. So the new cap, Massie took the new ball with Dennis Lillee against the established England opening pair, John Edrich and Geoff Boycott.

 ALAN McGILVRAY
And it's Massie to bowl again. No wicket for 22 and he's on his way now from the Nursery End to Boycott. Boycott, more sound in his approach to Massie than Edrich, smothering up, bat and pad close together, often very crouched in method, as he plays the balls going away from him. He's waiting for the next one and he has it and its bowled him! Right through him! He played forward, right over the top and the ball went right underneath the bat. I said he was playing more soundly, but he made a fibber of me there, didn't he? That's the first wicket with Boycott out for 11, bowled by Massie, good one, left him with movement in the air and he looses his wicket for 11, bowled by Massie.

ENGLAND
FIRST INNINGS
22-1

94

Bob Massie

Bob Massie

Lillee followed that wicket of Boycott with two other crucial blows, bowling Luckhurst for 1 and having Edrich lbw for 10 and it was 28 for 3. D'Oliveira and M.J.K. Smith stopped the rot to an extent, seeing England to lunch at 54 for 3. Massie accounted for both of them after the interval, though, D'Oliveira for 32 and Smith for 34. They had added 56 for the fourth wicket, but now England were in trouble again at 97 for 5.

Now came a pair who were to stage several revivals for England's batting in years to come, Alan Knott and Tony Greig. With the added encouragement of seeing Massie out of the attack with cramp in his leg, they pulled England gradually back into the game. They added 96 for the sixth wicket before Massie was able to return and induce Greig to slash at a wide one to be caught behind for 54. Seven runs later he had Knott caught at slip for 43. It was 200 for 7 and on his first day in Test cricket Bob Massie had taken five wickets.

With a new ball due after only two overs of the second day, Massie did not have to wait long to complete his demolition work. He took the last three wickets to finish with 8 for 84 and become only the third bowler in history to take eight on his Test debut. England were all out for 272, but the conditions still favoured the bowlers and John Snow and John Price almost immediately despatched the Australian openers, Bruce Francis and Keith Stackpole and it was 7 for 2. That brought the Chappell brothers together. Snow and Price determinedly fed the hook shot that had, of late, been Ian's downfall. So it was again today, but not before it had brought him a fair few runs and seen Australia through the worst of the crisis. Chappell caught at fine leg off Snow for 56; Australia 82 for 3, but brother Greg was still there. Doug Walters did not keep him company for long, he became another of Snow's victims, but the younger Chappell batted three hours before he hit a boundary. However he dominated play in what he rated as one of his best Test innings. Ross Edwards contributed only 28 to their fifth wicket stand of 106, and Chappell was still there, with the night watchman, Gleeson, in the last over of the day ...

AUSTRALIA
FIRST INNINGS
201-5

BRIAN JOHNSTON

So, just a little bit of tension at the end, this crowd of 29,000 have had a marvellous day. And here's Gifford now to Chappell — this one outside the off-stump and he's chopped that one up to third man and there'll be as many runs as he likes to take, up to three in this. Luckhurst has reached the ball now, short of the boundary and there're taking three and that means then he's got his 100 and Gleeson has one ball to play. There is still one ball remaining but some boys are running on from the Tavern to congratulate him. In fact, they've chosen the wrong end, they've come to pat Gleeson on the back and he will be very surprised about that.

It was Greg Chappell's second hundred against England and it continued until mid-morning on the third day. D'Oliveira was the one who finally breeched his defence, bowling him for 131. It was 250 for 7, but Rod Marsh now

Greg Chappell

hit out. He made 50 before being caught by Greig off Snow. During the lunch interval the weather changed ominously, becoming heavy and humid, on the edge of rain elsewhere in London. It helped Snow take his fifth wicket of the innings as Australia succumbed early in the afternoon with a lead of 36. Now Ian Chappell called for his fast bowlers to deliver him one England wicket before they re-took the lead. He was to get five.

It was Lillee who took the first two, including Boycott in remarkable fashion. Rather than dodge a shortish delivery which lifted, Boycott preferred to let it strike him, then could only watch in horror as it looped from his padded ribs over his shoulder and knock the off-bail. Soon afterwards Luckhurst was caught behind for 4 and it was 16 for 2, which rapidly became 18 for 3 when Massie had Edrich caught behind for 6. Thanks to catches by the Chappell brothers in the slips from D'Oliveira and Greig, Massie increased his haul for the match to 11 and England, at 31 for 5, were still five runs behind. The ball was seaming violently from Lillee, leaving dark green slurs on the pitch, and swinging extravagantly for Massie, but Mike Smith now dug in to provide the first resistance.

66 The conditions were ideal for Massie, but he really did use them well. The counter to his late swing was shown by Mike Smith (*right*) who was a very good technician and a thoughtful and analytical cricketer who really went into bowlers' methods, and he played a number of strokes that he worked out himself against particular types of bowling. **99**   **John Arlott**

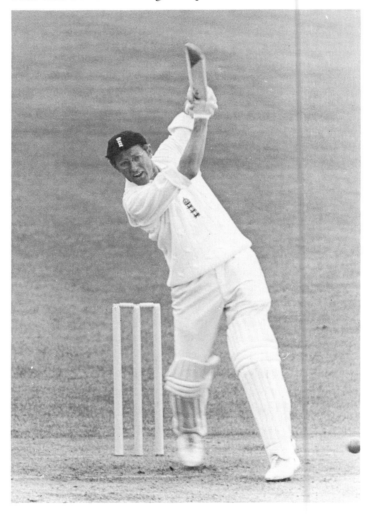

To counter the prodigious Massie swing, Smith made sure he was well across to the off side and came down the pitch to upset the length. With the score 52, Massie claimed the wicket of Knott for 12, but Illingworth stayed with Smith to add 22 for the seventh wicket …

JOHN ARLOTT
Massie, who's bowled unchanged throughout the innings, 20 overs now, taken 4 for 35 and he turns at the Nursery End, comes up, bowls and Illingworth edges that and he's caught! Caught by Stackpole at second slip who was one of those who'd had none of the booty until then. Massie's technique of sliding it across the right-hander has worked again and this is a record, of course. He's now on his own, taking 13 wickets in his first Test Match.

BILL FRINDALL
Five for 35 in this innings and no bowler, either in their first appearance in England v Australia matches or in their first Test, has taken 13 wickets.

John Snow immediately gave Massie his fourteenth wicket and Smith was running out of partners as that fateful Saturday afternoon session was near to the close …

ENGLAND
SECOND INNINGS
74-7

JOHN ARLOTT
Only two slips and a gully now for Smith and one hardly expected to see the close-catching field broken up in this innings. Up again comes Massie, bowls and Smith is out caught! Caught at square leg. Caught Edwards. He flicked at a full length in-swinger, sent it head high to Edwards who only had to clap his hands to catch it and that is 81 for 9.

ENGLAND
SECOND INNINGS
81-9

From that position it would have taken a miracle to have saved England and, despite a last wicket stand of 35 between John Price and Norman Gifford, it simply was not possible. On Monday morning Bob Massie took his eighth wicket of the innings again and England were all out for 116, leaving Australia only 81 runs to win. Bruce Francis and Ian Chappell fell cheaply enough, but after that it was a formality, with Keith Stackpole scoring the winning run in early afternoon for an eight wicket victory, achieved with nine and a half hours to spare.

For Bob Massie such a performance in his first Test was something to relish. He enjoyed the elation of his senior team-mates who had been starved of victory for over two years. Massie had taken 16 wickets for 137. Only two bowlers had done better in all Tests and this was by far the best on a debut, but Massie was only to play in another five Tests and that Lord's haul represented over half of his total of Test wickets.

66The atmosphere was so heavy. The ball swung to an incredible degree. Knott and Smith played him quite well but you just couldn't believe that he took wicket after wicket. He had this amazing ability to bowl an outswinger which went for miles and, in that atmosphere, it was money for old rope. He wasn't fast or anything. There is no explanation.99 **Brian Johnston**

66He didn't bowl anything like as well again. He bowled a good length, with a bit of swing and a bit of cut and he didn't take as many wickets in the rest of his Test career put together. I think he would have done well in county cricket, because he had plenty of stamina and plenty of strength and a good resilient temperament.99 **John Arlott**

Dennis Lillee

England and Australia won one more Test each in that series, to share the rubber two-apiece, so that England retained the Ashes. But in Australia's win at the Oval there was a sign for the future as a fast bowler took ten England wickets in the match. His name was D. K. Lillee.

Second Test, Lord's, 22-26 June 1972
Australia won by 8 wickets

ENGLAND

G. Boycott	b Massie	11	b Lillee		6
J. H. Edrich	lbw b Lillee	10	c Marsh b Massie		6
B. W. Luckhurst	b Lillee	1	c Marsh b Lillee		4
M. J. K. Smith	b Massie	34	c Edwards b Massie		30
B. L. D'Oliveira	lbw b Massie	32	c G. Chappell b Massie		3
A. W. Greig	c Marsh b Massie	54	c I. Chappell b Massie		3
†A. P. E. Knott	c Colley b Massie	43	c G. Chappell b Massie		12
*R. Illingworth	lbw b Massie	30	c Stackpole b Massie		12
J. A. Snow	b Massie	37	c Marsh b Massie		0
N. Gifford	c Marsh b Massie	3	not out		16
J. S. E. Price	not out	4	c G. Chappell b Massie		19
Extras	(lb6, w1, nb6)	13	(w1, nb4)		5
Total		**272**			**116**

AUSTRALIA

K. R. Stackpole	c Gifford b Price	5	not out		57
B. C. Francis	b Snow	0	c Knott b Price		9
*I. M. Chappell	c Smith b Snow	56	c Luckhurst b D'Oliveira	6
G. S. Chappell	b D'Oliveira	131	not out		7
K. D. Walters	c Illingworth b Snow	1			
R. Edwards	c Smith b Illingworth	28			
J. W. Gleeson	c Knott b Greig	1			
†R. W. Marsh	c Greig b Snow	50			
D. J. Colley	c Greig b Price	25			
R. A. L. Massie	c Knott b Snow	0			
D. K. Lillee	not out	2			
Extras	(lb7, nb2)	9	(lb2)		2
Total		**308**	(2 wkts)		**81**

BOWLING

AUSTRALIA	O	M	R	W		O	M	R	W
Lillee	28	3	90	2	–	21	6	50	2
Massie	32.5	7	84	8	–	27.2	9	53	8
Colley	16	2	42	0	–	7	1	8	0
G. Chappell	6	1	18	0	–				
Gleeson	9	1	25	0	–				
ENGLAND									
Snow	32	13	57	5	–	8	2	15	0
Price	26.1	5	87	2	–	7	0	28	1
Greig	29	6	74	1	–	3	0	17	0
D'Oliveira	17	5	48	1	–	8	3	14	1
Gifford	11	4	20	0	–				
Illingworth	7	2	13	1	–				
Luckhurst					–	0.5	0	5	0

ENGLAND fall of wickets
FIRST INNINGS: 1-22, 2-23, 3-28, 4-84, 5-97, 6-193, 7-200, 8-260, 9-265.
SECOND INNINGS: 1-12, 2-16, 3-18, 4-25, 5-31, 6-52, 7-74, 8-74, 9-81.
AUSTRALIA fall of wickets
FIRST INNINGS: 1-1, 2-7, 3-82, 4-84, 5-190, 6-212, 7-250, 8-290, 9-290.
SECOND INNINGS: 1-20, 2-51.

First Test at Old Trafford, June 8-13
England won by 89 runs
England 249 (Greig 57) and 234 (Greig 62, Lillee 6-66); Australia 142 (Stackpole 53) and 252 (Marsh 91, Stackpole 67).

Third Test at Trent Bridge, July 13-18
Match drawn
Australia 315 (Stackpole 114, Colley 54, Snow 5-92) and 324-4 dec (Edwards 170*, G. Chappell 72, I. Chappell 50); England 189 and 290-4 (Luckhurst 96, D'Oliveira 50*).

Fourth Test at Headingley, July 27-29
England won by 9 wickets
Australia 146 (Stackpole 52) and 136 (Underwood 6-45); England 263 (Illingworth 57, Mallett 5-114) and 21-1.

Fifth Test at The Oval, August 10-16
Australia won by 5 wickets
England 284 (Knott 92, Parfitt 51, Lillee 5-58) and 356 (Wood 90, Knott 63, Lillee 5-123); Australia 399 (I. Chappell 118, G. Chappell 113, Edwards 79) and 242-5 (Stackpole 79).

ENGLAND IN AUSTRALIA 1974/5

Commentators **Alan McGilvray, Christopher Martin-Jenkins, Dennis Cometti, Graham Dawson and Alan Marks**
Summariser **Lindsay Hassett**

"Ashes to Ashes, dust to dust – if Thomson don't get ya, Lillee must. . ."

The caption to Rigby's famous cartoon in the Sydney Sunday Telegraph told the story of England's demise against the pace and raw hostility of Dennis Lillee and Jeff Thomson. The battered and bewildered expression on the face of England's lion was an equally accurate description of the effects of their sustained bombardment during the winter of 1974/5. It was a combination that was to take England by storm – a confident England, too.

66Dennis Lillee was a very great fast bowler, without a shadow of doubt. And in his early days he carried a lot on his shoulders; he did not have a great deal of assistance – but then Jeff Thomson came along.99
John Arlott

Dennis Lillee (*left*) and Jeff Thomson (*right*)

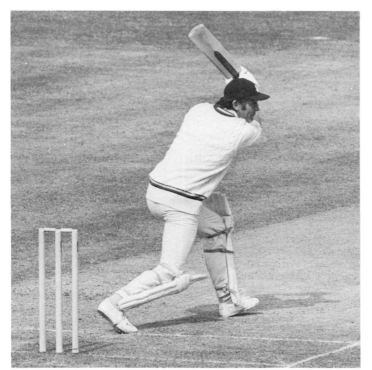

Perhaps as a result of some lack of faith in the leadership, Geoff Boycott had started a self-imposed exile from international cricket that was to last three years. So he was not in the MCC party which started their Australian tour with two wins against state sides. In the MCC victory over Queensland which immediately preceded the First Test on the same ground in Brisbane, the touring team had their first sight of Jeff Thomson.

❝He was more or less unknown. He had played in one Test and had been a disaster, so there was absolutely no advance warning. Thomson was just a name being muddled with 'Froggy' Thomson who played against Ray Illingworth's side. All that soon changed. In the Queensland match he bowled the first ball of the innings – it cut back and hit Dennis Amiss in the solar plexus and you could just see the shock on his face at the pace of the ball.
Thomson was very raw ... some of

the older heads thought he was quick but erratic. To some extent he was, but he had the great good fortune of bowling in the first Test on the Brisbane pitch which suited him.**99 Christopher Martin-Jenkins**

66There is one story that came out of Australia's first innings. Tony Greig got Dennis Lillee out with a bouncer and when Lillee came back into the dressing room he said to Ian Chappell, "Well, I want you to know now. They started it. But, by God, it's going to be me who finishes it." And when England batted we saw the sheer hostility and pace of Lillee and Thomson. And Lillee got quicker as he grew more confident about his back, while Thomson's brute force, the way he exploded the ball, was absolutely fearsome.**99**

Henry Blofeld

The Chappell brothers: Ian (above) and Greg (above right)

Ian Chappell obviously had enough faith in the pitch to bat when he won the toss and he played a large part himself in the recovery from 10 for 2 with a stand of exactly 100 with his brother. Ian made 90 and Greg 58 in Australia's 309 which owed a lot to some vigorous tail-wagging. The England bowlers, at this stage, were not afraid to dig the ball in short.

By the time British radio listeners joined the commentary on the second evening of the match, Thomson had already sent back Dennis Amiss and Brian Luckhurst, the England openers, for single figure scores.

CHRISTOPHER MARTIN-JENKINS
Well now for the first time since tea we're going to see Jeff Thomson coming on from the northern end and this is the end from which he did all the damage in his first explosive spell of 5 overs, 2 maidens, 2 for 4. He's got 2 for 18 at the moment and here he is coming in to bowl to Greig . . . and beats him, immediately, with a vicious delivery which lifted off a length. Greig was groping at thin air there, and the ball fairly whipped through to Marsh who is standing well back towards the sight screen at that far end.

LINDSAY HASSETT
I think that was just about as good a ball as he's bowled today. It was not only fast but it did move towards the slips. It swung a little and it really ripped off the pitch.

CHRISTOPHER MARTIN-JENKINS
Now Thomson is I would say, about 5 foot 10 inches in height, with long fair hair going quite a long way down his neck. This is only his second Test match. His first Test match was so unsuccessful that he didn't take any wickets, but he's had a big impact on this one. Thomson makes a slight adjustment to his bowling mark. He runs in off no more than 15 paces, a gentle run up to the wicket and then he almost stops and then this explosive last stride.

Edrich and Greig, with a fifth wicket stand of 73 which continued until the third morning, did bring respectability to the England first innings score. Indeed, after Edrich was caught at slip off Thomson for 48, Greig went on to reach an aggressive and defiant century and, with help from the tail, to reduce the Australian lead to 44.

Starting their innings on the third evening, Australia were able to declare, leaving England forty minutes to bat on the fourth day and all of the fifth and a target of 333, which might, with a good start, be tempting. In the event bad light and the breakdown of the motor roller restricted their batting that evening to just two overs, but starting the final day at 10 for no wicket, they must have felt they had a chance of survival at least. Jeff Thomson had other ideas, though. He took two wickets in successive overs before lunch, which was taken at 80 for 3. His next burst reduced England to 94 for 6 and soon it was 115 for 7 with the tea interval still to come. Underwood, as he had in the first innings, resisted bravely, but soon after his dismissal came the coup de grace. . .

ALAN McGILVRAY
9 wickets for 166 and an hour and just over 20 minutes left in this the last day's play in this First Test at Brisbane in Queensland.
With Thomson, the breeze favouring him a little, coming in over his left shoulder, and he's using it very well indeed, bringing the ball in a little bit for the most part. He goes in to bowl to Hendrick. And Hendrick plays at it and that lifted, caught him on the finger of the right hand. He's rubbing his hand but it came up from a pretty good length to lift sharply. He made it pretty awkward for himself by walking away, and

ENGLAND
FIRST INNINGS
75-4

**ENGLAND
SECOND INNINGS
166 all out**

66Thomson never tried to do anything other than bowl fast. He didn't try to do anything with the ball. He didn't need to. With his sheer pace and, on that pitch in particular, bounce off a length in the second innings when the track had started to go, he really was as close to being unplayable as I've ever seen.

They all approached it in different ways. Greig had successfully attacked with a great barnstorming hundred but I personally think that was counter-productive in the end because the rest of them rather tended to think that the reckless way was the only way.99
Christopher Martin-Jenkins

Colin Cowdrey

the ball kept coming in toward him and it struck him on the finger. He's all right now and all set for Thomson to move in again and bowl. And Hendrick, . . . bowled him! And that's the end of the match. He walked away from it. It ran through a little bit low, finished about three-quarter stump high and that's the end of the Test match with Australia winning the First Test. So, Thomson took his sixth wicket when he bowled Hendrick without scoring and England are all out for 166, all out 166.

Thomson had taken 6 for 46, and 9 wickets in the match, while Lillee and Walker had taken four apiece.

Listening to the early morning commentaries from Brisbane in the comfort and safety of his own home had been Colin Cowdrey. As the team flew across the island continent to Perth for the Second Test, Cowdrey received the call to duty which, as he approached his 42nd birthday after three and a half years absence from Test cricket, he could hardly have been expecting. But, with Edrich's hand and Amiss's thumb broken he answered that call and arrived in Perth in time to see the MCC's defeat at the hands of Western Australia. Four days later, when England had been put in to bat and Luckhurst had been dismissed for 27, Cowdrey was walking out to bat in a Test match again.

Cowdrey had come in at 44 for 1 and with David Lloyd he took the score to 99. He was bowled behind his legs, moving too far across to Thomson – not a common fault by English batsmen in this series – for 22. Thomson had also had Lloyd caught at slip for 49, but England's encouraging start was not sustained, despite Knott's 51 and by the end of the first day Australia were batting in reply to England's 208 all out. This time Lillee, Thomson and Walker had each taken 2 wickets, as had that useful change bowler Doug Walters in only 2½ overs.

It was Walters who was to steal the show on the second day, taking the game away from England after tea with a dazzling display which outshone the substantial contributions of Redpath, Wally Edwards, the Chappells and even his partner in a fifth wicket stand of 170, Ross Edwards . . .

AUSTRALIA
FIRST INNINGS
352-4

ENGLAND
SECOND INNINGS
52-0

CHRISTOPHER MARTIN-JENKINS
So the last ball of the day. Walters 97 not out. 346 for 4 wickets, Australia. Three forty five runs in the day so far. Those schoolboys almost over the boundary's edge ready to sprint on. Here comes Willis. He bowls to Walters. Walters hooks and it's four runs! No it's six! It's six! Over the top of the schoolboys who started off onto the field. The two umpires going over to check up, I think, whether that was six but anyway umpire Bailhache has signalled six. Umpire Tom Brooks going over to see. Either way it doesn't really matter, because with the last ball of the day, Doug Walters has got his hundred and just listen to the applause.

That six off the last ball of the second day had given Walters exactly a hundred in the session, the second time in his Test career that he had achieved that feat. He did not add to his overnight 103. Ross Edwards went on to a century, making 115, but, despite 41 from Marsh, Australia's 481 was not quite the score they had at one stage threatened.

Brian Luckhurst, hit on the hand in the first innings, was not able to open and there was an inevitability about the choice of his replacement for the second innings. It was the man whose arrival had inspired the Australian cartoonists to suggest that England's next replacement would be WG Grace – Colin Cowdrey. Again, he enjoyed a useful stand with David Lloyd, taking the score past fifty for the first wicket . . .

CHRISTOPHER MARTIN-JENKINS
Still Thomson from the river end, bowling to Lloyd, who's hit on, oohh hit nastily here and that really is going to hurt poor David Lloyd. It hit him in the place where it hurts and he's quite clearly in agony. He's folded over, completely collapsed onto the gound and the whole Australian side is now circling round him. That one whipped through from just short of a length, Lloyd took the bat away and it hit him where it hurts and really I can almost feel that up here. He's up on his feet but he is very unhappy indeed. He is staggering on his feet at the moment and they're carrying him away from the pitch and this really is . . . my goodness this is a tough game when you're up against fast bowlers like this . . .

108

Thomson comes in, bowls to Cowdrey and this time he gets it away off his toes. This'll be four runs down past the short leg. Scatters the seagulls again. The ball fielded by the Australian 12th man Jenner who is down beyond the boundary in front of the pavilion waiting to hand out drinks to the players. With him there, John Edrich. Thomson goes back to his mark and here he comes now running in again to bowl to Cowdrey. Cowdrey gets a ball which hits him on the pad and he's give out lbw! Lbw for 41. So the first England wicket falls and Colin Cowdrey, having done a marvellous job, is lbw to Thomson for 41. England are 62 for 1 and just listen to this applause for Cowdrey. And as you listen to it consider that, just a week ago, Cowdrey was at home in a cold English December. I've got Alec Bedser now sitting in the box. I'm sure Alec, Cowdrey has done everything that could possibly have been asked of him.

ALEC BEDSER
Yes, Chris. Well he's done more than you could possibly hope for because he really didn't think it was possible to play in the game at all so soon after coming out. But, well, you're just forced to do it but he's responded magnificently and he's shown what great technique he's got.

That wicket of Cowdrey was the only one England lost on that fourth day, so again they started the final day with a fair chance of saving the game. They were 102 for 1, with Lloyd able to resume at the fall of the next wicket. The first target was to 273 to make Australia bat again.

As in Brisbane, though, it was Thomson who shattered the dreams with the wickets of the overnight batsmen, Denness and Greig, and then Fletcher for a duck, in his first three overs of the day. England were 124 for 4. Lillee sent back Knott and, though the two casualties of the match, Lloyd and Luckhurst, did their brave best, it was only an innings by Fred Titmus, exactly one month older than Cowdrey, that held up Australia.

DENNIS COMETTI
Mallett continues a new over, bowling to Titmus who goes forward, playing the ball out on the off side. No run. I'll get the figures on Thomson. 25 overs, his figures 5 for 93. Mallett bowling his 12th over. In again to Titmus, the second

Jeff Thomson

ball of the over brings Titmus forward on the drive. He could be caught at long off. He is! Diving catch by Greg Chappell. That's a record breaking catch. He's taken more catches in this match than any one else for Australia in Test history. Titmus caught Chappell, bowled Mallett for 61. England all out 293, giving them a lead of 20. Australia have to bat again, requiring 20 runs to win the Second Test.

The target was reached for the loss of just one wicket and Australia were 2-0 up in the series.

England arrived in Melbourne for Christmas after a narrowly drawn game against South Australia. The start of the Third Test, running from Boxing Day to New Year's Eve, seemed to be the same old story. Thomson with four wickets, and Lillee with two, bowled England out for 242. But then a hostile Bob Willis took 5 wickets to win for England a first innings lead – albeit of just a single run. This slender advantage was splendidly built on by Amiss and Lloyd with an opening partnership of 115 of which Lloyd made 44. Amiss went on to make 90, but there came another English collapse of surprising suddenness, though Greig, as swashbuckling as ever, made 60.

All out for 244, England had set Australia 246 to win. They had made 4 of them when the final day began. The England attack had lost Mike Hendrick with a pulled hamstring, but had been encouraged by the four wickets captured by off spinner, Ashley Mallett. Fred Titmus was likely to be a key figure. With the new ball, Greig and Willis gave England a great start, removing Wally Edwards and Ian Chappell for ducks and it was 5 for 2. Then Redpath and Greg Chappell swung the pendulum back towards Australia with a stand of 101, before Redpath was run out for 39 and Chappell lbw to Titmus for 61. England seized back the initiative now with Titmus' second wicket and it was 121 for 5. However, Doug Walters, batting with Rod Marsh, stood firm …

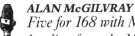 **ALAN McGILVRAY**
Five for 168 with Marsh 13 and Walters 32. Greig, bowling from the Member's Stand end. He has the left hander, Marsh, in strike. Marsh hits it hard on the on side … they've run three as Underwood throws a long and wide

return to Knott. That brings it to 5 for 171.
There's real excitement here now with Australia making the decision, win or lose, but do it well, whatever they do. And this attitude is good. They're after the runs, they're taking the risks. If they fail, well, England will win. Now, Greig bowls to Walters and he drives it uppishly . . . and he's caught!

AUSTRALIA
SECOND INNINGS
171-5

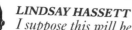 **LINDSAY HASSETT**
I suppose this will be the testing point as to the attitude of the captains. Australia, now 75 runs short of their target and somewhere round about 23 overs to be bowled.

As the last hour started it seemed that both sides had gone on the defensive. But at last Denness decided to take the initiative and the new ball, which awoke Rod Marsh into attack again. At 208 he fell for 40, but now Max Walker was joined by Lillee and the assault continued.

Fourteen runs were needed off the last two overs and Underwood bowled a fine, tight maiden over to Lillee.

 CHRISTOPHER MARTIN-JENKINS
It's 235 for 7. 4 balls to go, 11 to win. Greig from the Southern end. Bowls to Lillee. Lillee hits it. It's up in the air. It's going towards Denness! He catches it at extra cover and Lillee is out! Lillee, perishing gloriously in the cause and now, with 3 balls left, Australia have 11 to win and England have to get 2 wickets to try and win the match. Lillee out for 14.

 LINDSAY HASSETT
Three deliveries to go now. Max Walker has the strike. Australia still require 10 runs to tie, 11 runs to win this game. It's asking too much I would think to get 11 from the 3 deliveries and I would think that Max Walker will probably play them quietly.

AUSTRALIA
SECOND INNINGS
235-8

Three more runs did come, leaving Australia 8 runs and England two wickets short in a tantalising draw.

The only match before the Fourth Test in Sydney was a one day international which England won, but, before the Test team was chosen, the England captain, Mike Denness made the momentous decision to stand down. His scores of 8 and 2 in Melbourne had taken his tally in six Test innings to 65, a slightly better average than Keith Fletcher who had 40 from 4 innings and who now returned after missing the Melbourne Test.

66 Denness had not been well at the start of the tour and they were quite worried about what was wrong with him. He had these mysterious back pains and they tested him extensively. He recovered and was fine after the Tests but he just couldn't put an innings together and his technique was found a little wanting by the quicker bowlers. **99**

Christopher Martin-Jenkins

66 I think the targeting of the captain is a deliberate policy. Once you've undermined the captain's ability to bat, you've then sent serious doubts throughout the side. As soon as the captain starts thinking he should stand down, the side is at a tremendous disadvantage. And Thomson and Lillee certainly did this to Denness. **99**   **Henry Blofeld**

Denness falls victim to Max Walker

So, on January 4, it was John Edrich who went out to toss with Ian Chappell. This time Chappell chose to bat and his new opener Rick McCosker did him proud, making 80. Runs came steadily for the next day and a half and Australia made 405.

Lillee, Thomson and Walker now got to work and looked likely to enforce a follow-on at 123 for 5, but Edrich was sound and imperturbable, batting at 4, and made 50, joined by Knott in a stand of 57 for the sixth wicket. Knott's puckish improvisation took him to a splendid 82 and his seventh wicket partnership of 60 with Titmus saw the follow-on comfortably avoided. Centuries by Greg Chappell and Redpath enabled Australia to set England 400 to win, or, more realistically, four sessions to survive. Rain trimmed that to nearer three sessions but on the last day Lillee, Thomson and Walker soon made it 74 for 3. Worse still, Edrich had taken his first ball from Lillee just below the rib cage and was sent to hospital. Thomson had Fletcher caught at slip for 11 after shaking him up with a short ball which he deflected onto his head and Greig flailed 54. At 156 for 6 Edrich returned and soon found himself partnering his No.10, Willis . . .

ALAN McGILVRAY
Now it's a beautiful, beautiful afternoon here in Sydney. The sun shining and all those storm clouds have passed away to our right. Well, England fighting very hard to save this game.

We have the third over of the last 15 overs now being bowled and only 2 wickets to fall. Chappell, I think, is beginning to get a little worried. This defence has been very good. Here is Willis against Lillee. Now here is Lillee moving in and going in very quickly as he bowls to Willis and it's straight on line. He's bowled him! He's out bowled. Willis is out bowled by Lillee. It looked to be inevitable but I pay full credit to Willis. He'll get a great hand from this crowd, I'm sure. That was a good ball, it curved away a little from him and he walked away, came back too late and the ball ran into his stumps and so 9 wickets are down for 201.

Lillee in full flight, taking his second wicket, for 62. He's bowling his nineteenth over. Edrich is 24 and 12 overs and a few balls yet to be bowled, too, if this match is to be saved. Now here's Lillee to bowl to Arnold and Arnold gets a nasty one. It flies over his head, over the keeper's head and goes away for 4 byes. That was very short. I see no reason why those deliveries should be bowled at last wicket batsmen. I've said it before, I don't think it's necessary but Lillee inclined to bounce that one and he did. It was a nasty one but Arnold just looked at it go. It went straight over his head and I note now Lillee is being spoken to by umpire Bailhache. And he's been warned that this will not happen. Lillee hands on hips. No, I agree with umpire Bailhache. He's been told before.

ALAN MARKS
Arnold moves to 14, Edrich 33, 9 for 228. This is the tenth over of the last 15 to be bowled. Mallett to Arnold, coming forward and caught! Yes, caught by Greg Chappell at short forward leg and the Ashes are Australia's for the first time since 1971 when Ray Illingworth took them home. The last man out was Arnold, caught Greg Chappell bowled Mallett for 14. Ashley Mallett wins the series for Australia and the Ashes with his 100th wicket in Test cricket.

In the Fifth Test in Adelaide, Dennis Lillee really came into his own, despite the loss of his comrade in arms,

ENGLAND
SECOND INNINGS
201-9

ENGLAND
SECOND INNINGS
228 all out

Thomson, to a rest day shoulder injury sustained playing tennis. Lillee's 4 wickets in each innings gave Australia victory, though there were England heroics from Underwood, with 11 wickets in the match, and Knott with a gallant second innings hundred.

The final Test, back in Melbourne, at last saw England's revenge. With Thomson still unfit and Lillee limping off with a damaged heel after nine overs, England made hay after Lever's six wickets had dismissed Australia for 152. Denness and Fletcher each made big hundreds and an innings victory merely underlined that the difference between the sides was the phenomenal impact of Lillee and Thomson.

66For one or two of the tailenders it became fear. Geoff Arnold came within a quarter of an inch of being killed by Lillee in Sydney. Keith Fletcher, in Sydney, gloved a ball onto his forehead and it bounced out almost as far as Ross Edwards who just failed to catch it at cover point. He was out next ball, looking absolutely white as a sheet, so I think you could say that was fear at work.**99**
Christopher Martin-Jenkins

66Thomson was just very quick but Lillee was a great bowler. I describe him as the last of the great Australian bowlers. He had a very good action and a fine, loose run-up. He was not the best ever – he didn't have Lindwall's pace or accuracy but a very fine bowler indeed.
They exposed the fact that our batsmen's technique was lacking. Our batsmen just couldn't cope. Some of them were playing at the ball from so far away they were lucky to get a touch and I think some of them, in the end were happy to get out because they were frightened.**99**   **Fred Trueman**

Titmus, bowled over by Thomson

First Test, Brisbane, 29 November-4 December 1974
Australia won by 166 runs

AUSTRALIA

I. R. Redpath b Willis	5	b Willis	25
W. J. Edwards c Amiss b Hendrick	4	c Knott b Willis	5
*I. M. Chappell c Greig b Willis	90	c Fletcher b Underwood	11
G. S. Chappell c Fletcher b Underwood	58	b Underwood	71
R. Edwards c Knott b Underwood	32	c Knott b Willis	53
K. D. Walters c Lever b Willis	3	not out	62
†R. W. Marsh c Denness b Hendrick	14	not out	46
T. J. Jenner c Lever b Willis	12		
D. K. Lillee c Knott b Greig	15		
M. H. N. Walker not out	41		
J. R. Thomson run out	23		
Extras (lb4, nb8)	12	(b1, lb7, w1, nb6)	15
Total	309	(5 wkts dec)	288

ENGLAND

D. L. Amiss c Jenner b Thomson	7	c Walters b Thomson	25
B. W. Luckhurst c Marsh b Thomson	1	c I. Chappell b Lillee	3
J. H. Edrich c I. Chappell b Thomson	48	b Thomson	6
*M. H. Denness lbw b Walker	6	c Walters b Thomson	27
K. W. R. Fletcher b Lillee	17	c G. Chappell b Jenner	19
A. W. Greig c Marsh b Lillee	110	b Thomson	2
†A. P. E. Knott c Jenner b Walker	12	b Thomson	19
P. Lever c I. Chappell b Walker	4	c Redpath b Lillee	14
D. L. Underwood c Redpath b Walters	25	c Walker b Jenner	30
R. G. D. Willis not out	13	not out	3
M. Hendrick c Redpath b Walker	4	b Thomson	0
Extras (b5, lb2, w3, nb8)	18	(b8, lb3, w2, nb5)	18
Total	265		166

BOWLING

ENGLAND	O	M	R	W		O	M	R	W
Willis	21.5	3	56	4	–	15	3	45	3
Lever	16	1	53	0	–	18	4	58	0
Hendrick	19	3	64	2	–	13	2	47	0
Greig	16	2	70	1	–	13	2	60	0
Underwood	20	6	54	2	–	26	6	63	2
AUSTRALIA									
Lillee	23	6	73	2	–	12	2	25	2
Thomson	21	5	59	3	–	17.5	3	46	6
Walker	24.5	2	73	4	–	9	4	32	0
Walters	6	1	18	1	–	2	2	0	0
Jenner	6	1	24	0	–	16	5	45	2

AUSTRALIA fall of wickets
FIRST INNINGS: 1-7, 2-10, 3-110, 4-197, 5-202, 6-205, 7-228, 8-229, 9-257.
SECOND INNINGS: 1-15, 2-39, 3-59, 4-173, 5-190.
ENGLAND fall of wickets
FIRST INNINGS: 1-9, 2-10, 3-33, 4-57, 5-130, 6-162, 7-168, 8-226, 9-248.
SECOND INNINGS: 1-18, 2-40, 3-44, 4-92, 5-94, 6-94, 7-115, 8-162, 9-163.

Second Test at Perth, December 13-17
Australia won by 9 wickets
England 208 (Knott 51) and 293 (Titmus 61, Thomson 5-93); Australia 481 (R. Edwards 115, Walters 103, G. Chappell 62) and 23-1.

Third Test at Melbourne, December 26-31
Match drawn
England 242 (Knott 52) and 244 (Amiss 90, Greig 60); Australia 241 (Redpath 55, Willis 5-61) and 238-8 (G. Chappell 61)

Fourth Test at Sydney, January 4-9
Australia won by 171 runs
Australia 405 (G. Chappell 84, McCosker 80, I. Chappell 53, Arnold 5-86) and 289-4 dec (G. Chappell 144, Redpath 105); England 295 (Knott 82, Edrich 50) and 228 (Greig 54).

Fifth Test at Adelaide, January 25-30
Australia won by 163 runs
Australia 304 (Jenner 74, Walters 55, Underwood 7-113) and 272-5 dec (Walters 71*, Marsh 55, Redpath 52); England 172 (Denness 51) and 241 (Knott 106*, Fletcher 63).

Sixth Test at Melbourne, February 8-13
England won by an innings and 4 runs
Australia 152 (I. Chappell 65, P. Lever 6-38) and 373 (G. Chappell 102, Redpath 83, McCosker 76, I. Chappell 50); England 529 (Denness 188, Fletcher 146, Greig 89, Edrich 70, Walker 8-143).

115

AUSTRALIA IN ENGLAND 1975

The Second Test, **Lords,** *July 31-August 5*
The Third Test, **Headingley,** *August 14-19*
Commentators **John Arlott, Brian Johnston, Alan McGilvray and Alan Gibson**
Summarisers **Trevor Bailey and Fred Trueman**

The arrangement of a four Test series to follow the first World Cup competition might have seemed just a bit too much of a bad thing to English batsmen after the previous winter's battering. Indeed, the first Test at Edgbaston proved to be business as usual for Lillee, Thomson and Walker.

Denness put Australia in, possibly to avoid a first day humiliation for his batsmen, but then, in reply to a substantial Australian total, England were caught on a wet pitch and defeated by an innings. It was an inauspicious beginning to Graham Gooch's test career – he bagged a pair on his debut.

A dramatic new approach was needed and the selectors responded by appointing a new captain. Tony Greig came in to replace Denness and he set about choosing the men to turn the tide . . .

66 Greig realised that he needed somebody to blunt the Australian attack. He rang Ray Illingworth and Brian Close, and asked: "What the hell are we going to do?". They both, independently, suggested David Steele. He was a stodgy kind of batsman — the type who tend never to be noticed.
The atmosphere changed — Greig was a very inspirational type of character and his attitude was right for the occasion. He was worth his place as a player to a greater extent than was Mike Denness. **99** **Don Mosey**

Four men with a mission: (Left to right) David Steele, Bob Woolmer, Phil Edmonds (debutant at Leeds) and Tony Greig

The other new name on Greig's list was Bob Woolmer, regarded as a useful all-rounder. At Lord's, the sun was shining and England won the toss. Very quickly, though, it looked as if nothing else had changed . . .

JOHN ARLOTT

Lillee, bowling with the wind directly behind him, moves up, bowls to Wood and Wood is lbw, moving across. It came back, he is looking back in doubt or disappointment but he is out. I think he thought that was going to leave him.

TREVOR BAILEY

Lillee is quick. I mean this is the point I think some people do not appreciate. He is very quick indeed, he is much quicker than shall we say Snow, Lever or Old. Wood was understandably late on the shot. It nipped back, hit him on the right leg and that was thank you very much indeed.

And, coming in now we have Steele playing in his first Test match. Now this really is a toughy. But he is a tough little man, full of guts; a little bit limited in his stroke making, but he does believe in staying there.

David Steele had never before changed in the home dressing room at Lord's and lost his way as he was going out to bat, finding himself by the gents in the basement. The incoming batsman, Barry Wood had to direct him through the Long Room out into the sunshine.

Wood trapped by Lillee

ENGLAND
FIRST INNINGS
10-1

66 Clive Taylor wrote that marvellous line in the Sun, that Steele eventually emerged "looking like a bank clerk going to war." He was one of those marvellously romantic characters that history throws up from time to time. Someone who, on the face of it, has not a hope in hell and never looked likely to get a chance, but having been given that chance, seized it in both hands. 99

Henry Blofeld

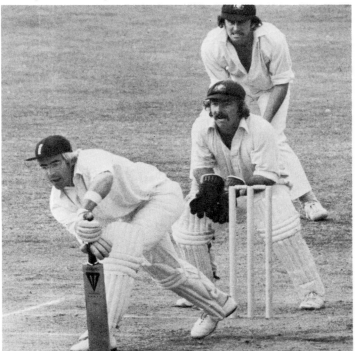

David Steele

ENGLAND
FIRST INNINGS
39-3

ENGLAND
FIRST INNINGS
43-3

ENGLAND
FIRST INNINGS
49-4

JOHN ARLOTT

His hair is prematurely grey showing quite strikingly under the cap. He plays in glasses, a good sticker with some punishing strokes especially in front of the wicket, he tends rather to play off the front foot. That did not do Tom Graveney any harm but it is not always an asset against bowlers of this pace.

Steele soon found himself in the midst of a crisis as Lillee had both Edrich and Amiss lbw.

ALAN McGILVRAY

The score is now 3 for 35 with Gooch one and Steele 12. Lillee moving in to Steele … that is a nice clip shot for 4 runs, a beautiful one. That was short, he moved inside, positioned himself well, went forward and then back, had time enough to do that, the ball was very short and punched it hard past backward square leg, picked its line up and hit it right in the middle of the bat for 4 to bring his score to 16.

ALAN McGILVRAY

Now Lillee bowling again to Steele. Steele forward to glide it away past point and Mallett chasing. They have run one, this will be close …, I think it will be 4. McCosker is chasing but he cannot get it.

Here at last was something for all England to cheer. Gooch became Lillee's fourth victim at 49, but Greig was just the man for the moment as he strode out to join Steele …

FRED TRUEMAN

I am sure Dennis Lillee must be thinking to himself I can bowl this England side out on any wicket I want to and any time I want.

JOHN ARLOTT

That applause is for Tony Greig, his first match as England's captain. Here he is, doing a little arm circling, wearing very heavily padded batting gloves, walking out, that slightly pin-toed walk, long legged, well over six feet tall, fair haired and coming out with England, once more, in crisis. In fact he can hardly remember, I shouldn't think, when he did not come in with England in crisis.

As we have so often seen, it was a partnership of completely contrasting styles that started to help England out of that crisis …

Tony Greig

 BRIAN JOHNSTON
This partnership worth 83 and it has only been about 86 minutes, the time of Greig's innings. The 37th over this is — 132 for 4, and they came together in the seventeenth. Well, 48 to Greig, is he going to be the first to get his 50? And Lillee at the moment 4 for 62, as he comes in now past umpire Bill Alley, bowls to Greig … Greig turns this one down … This is his fifty, is it? … or not? … Walker running in below us under the Warner stand … they are coming for the second … The throw is going for the stumps and it in fact just takes off the bail. Marsh did not take it, but it just hit the stumps, and Greig has got his fifty! (Cheers and applause). A lucky England captain. By that I mean he captains his first Test; he wins the toss; he comes in and with all his skill he plays an absolutely splendid innings. And this is the ingredient that England have badly wanted.

 FRED TRUEMAN
Oh, he has played very well indeed. He has played some real shots of authority.

 BRIAN JOHNSTON
Seventy-five balls, 87 minutes and 8 fours and some really lovely ones.

FRED TRUEMAN
It is so refreshing and so reassuring for English cricket lovers to see that at last England are taking the fight to the Australians and doing something about it, and nobody better than Greig. He has played magnificently since he came in.

BRIAN JOHNSTON
Well, Steele needing one more for his 50. Mallett comes up and bowls to him, it is short and he clips that away and that is going to be one run only, to mid wicket, but it is his 50, as it is fielded by McCosker in front of the Mound stand (Applause). And Steele takes off his cap. Reveals to those who do not know him the blueish grey hair which is underneath his cap and this is a 50 in his first Test match. Steele is 50. Ninety-nine balls as opposed to Greig's 75, 158 minutes and 9 fours. Well done, David Steele.

Steele did not stay much longer. Ian Chappell brought back Jeff Thomson, who had been plagued by overstepping, and he bowled the new England hero for 50.

ENGLAND
FIRST INNINGS
134-4

ENGLAND
FIRST INNINGS
143-4

But Steele returned to a rapturous ovation after sharing a fifth wicket stand of 96. The recovery was continued by Alan Knott who helped Greig add 77 for the sixth wicket and to the verge of his century ...

BRIAN JOHNSTON
He waits now and the bat will be coming up in a minute as Walker bowls. It does and Walker bowls ... and he is caught! He is caught at slip, he is caught by Ian Chappell! Greig is out for 96 caught Ian Chappell bowled Walker, they come in ... Oh, I thought they were coming in to tea, I do not know why ... oh, they are all going over to congratulate Ian Chappell! So England, 222 for 6, and England's captain out for 96 and the whole ground stands to cheer him back into the pavilion. He takes his cap off. Let us listen to this applause ...

**ENGLAND
FIRST INNINGS
222-6**

TREVOR BAILEY
Well Brian, I must confess I am very sorry because if ever I have seen a hundred deserved that was it. It was a splendid innings both in the way it was played and in the timing, the situation, the fact he was captaining ... you simply could not ask for more, it was absolutely first class.

Knott went on to make 69 and the other new cap, Woolmer, 33, to help England to an eventual total of 315.

John Snow gave England a tremendous start, causing mayhem in the Australian ranks on that Friday morning, dismissing Alan Turner and the Chappell brothers with only 37 runs on the board. Peter Lever joined in with the wickets of McCosker and Walters and, in the early afternoon, when Greig sent back Marsh, and Snow bowled Walker for his fourth wicket, it was 81 for 7. There was an Australian revival underway, Ross Edwards who was playing some fine shots put on 52 for the eighth wicket with Jeff Thomson. Then he received some enterprising assistance from Dennis Lillee ...

John Snow

BRIAN JOHNSTON
And Greig making it as difficult as possible, quite rightly, for Ross Edwards to get this ton which is going to be one of the best innings one has seen for a long time. He came in when the score was what, 37 for 3. He is there waiting as Woolmer comes up, bowls this to him, oh my goodness, he is out! He is out lbw yorked ... or was it bowled? It must have been lbw.

Yes, yorked lbw on 99. Oh dear me, how awful! But he is getting the same reception he would have done had he got a hundred. Yorked by Woolmer, Woolmer's first wicket in Test cricket and alas, poor Ross Edwards, out for 99.

FRED TRUEMAN

Wonderful innings by Ross Edwards which really has put Australia back into a position they could never have expected at one time. And once more I am going to give credit to Tony Greig who kept the field tight, credit to young Bob Woolmer who bowled a very good over, made Ross Edwards play at every delivery and really put the pressure on him. It was a fine bit of captaincy, a fine bit of bowling and, sadly, an end to a very, very good innings.

Australia were by no means finished, even now. Lillee started to attack the England bowling in fine style, hitting three sixes in a last wicket stand of 69 which restricted England's first innings lead to 47. Lillee was left 73 not out when David Steele, with his fourth ball in Test cricket ended the innings at 268.

The Saturday, with the gates closed at Lord's for the third time, was given to accumulation by England. They lost only two wickets, Wood for 52 and Steele for 45 while adding to their lead by 230. At the heart of it was John Edrich …

ALAN McGILVRAY

It is still one for 213. Two-hundred and eight on the day, they have about 33 minutes to go. It has been fairly slow, it has been a fairly slow scoring rate hasn't it?

TREVOR BAILEY

Well it has when one takes into account this is a very fast scoring ground.

ALAN McGILVRAY

I am not blaming Edrich now. Certainly I'd like to see him get his hundred but after that we should see some movement into attack. Lillee goes in to bowl to Edrich and Edrich turns it down to fine leg and there is his hundred I am sure. He will have to go quickly, this is close, he is home, he is home! That is the hundred for Edrich! Walker came in quickly, sent the return back but Edrich simply flew to make that second run and just got home in time.

AUSTRALIA
FIRST INNINGS
199-9

John Edrich

ENGLAND
SECOND INNINGS
215-1

121

It was John Edrich's seventh hundred against Australia and when he was eventually caught at long-on off Mallett for 175, Greig was trying to force the pace. He made 41 and, after his departure, was deciding about a declaration in late afternoon, when there was an unusual interruption …

JOHN ARLOTT
So Woolmer 6, Knott 11, England 399 for 6, 446 in front by Bill Frindall's calculator and my mental arithmetic. There are some signals going on to the dressing room, Woolmer is running in, lots of people are running out. Old is bringing Woolmer what, a glass of water. Unusual … and a freaker!* We have got a freaker* down the wicket now, not very shapely as it is masculine and I would think it has seen the last of its cricket for the day. The police are mustered, so are the cameramen and Greg Chappell. No! He has had his load, he is being embraced by a blond policeman and this may be his last public appearance. But what a splendid one. And so warm! Many, of course, have done this on cold rugby grounds but this chap has done it before 25,000 people on a day when he does not even feel cold, and he is now being marched down in the final exhibition past at least 8,000 people in the Mound stand some of whom, perhaps, have never seen anything quite like this before.
*N.B. freaker = streaker.

John Arlott's "Freaker"

ENGLAND
SECOND INNINGS
399-6

Greig's calculations brought him to a declaration at 436 for 7 just before tea on that fourth day. There was euphoria in the land and certainly, spirits had been restored, even though a combination of staunch Australian batting and a little rain on the last morning helped Australia to a comfortable draw.

The renaissance was to be carried on to the third Test at Headingley, where England made four changes, switching the balance of the bowling attack from seam to spin by introducing another slow left-armer to partner Underwood in Phillippe Edmonds. Australia, though, chose to go the other way, remembering a sensational piece of left-arm swing bowling on this ground by Gary Gilmour in the World Cup. To make room for him, Marsh was promoted to open the innings in place of Turner. Greig won the toss, and after 35 minutes of the first day, two stalwarts of the Lord's Test were together in a century stand for the second wicket – Edrich and Steele. It was to be a particularly valuable innings for Steele, who had met a meat trader in the Northamptonshire committee room the week before and been promised a lamb chop for each run he made up to 50 and a steak a run thereafter. He was onto steaks before Edrich departed for 62 after a stand of 112 and, when he eventually fell to Thomson for 73, his sponsor was on the telephone begging him to go easy in the second innings.

England finished the first day at 251 for 5. Greig reached his half century early on the second, England collapsed to Gilmour for 288. Australia were back in the game, but if, at that stage, Gilmour had taken the honours with six wickets, it was the England debutant who was to steal the back page headlines. With the score 77 for 2 Greig introduced Edmonds …

ALAN GIBSON *He's a tall, fair, good looking young man.*

TREVOR BAILEY *Good looking bowler too.*

ALAN GIBSON
He has style about all his play, I think. Bowls again. Oh that's tremendous. Chappell plays and misses and is bowled. So that's Edmonds' first wicket. Greig rushes up and claps him on the back and away goes Chappell, 78 for 3. Ian Chappell it was. He got 35 and, with the captain gone, things must look decidedly brighter for England.

TREVOR BAILEY
Well, we've said he's bowled well and so, typically, he undoubtedly got his wicket with undoubtedly the worst ball he's bowled. It was a short long hop which went … not straight along the ground, but kept very low indeed.

ALAN GIBSON
Well, now, in comes Edwards and Edmonds will be bowling to him and we've got three slips. Greig has come to that position on the off side, silly point in front of the bat again, and a short leg. So there are five men all very close to the bat. As Edmonds comes in and bowls to Edwards. Hits him on the pad … and he's out! Well now I wonder will it prove to have been Edwards' misfortune to come in in the middle of a hat-trick. Anyway that's 78 for 4.

Phil Edmonds

AUSTRALIA
FIRST INNINGS
78-4

Two wickets for Edmonds in his second over in Test cricket. What could he do in his third?

ALAN GIBSON
Two slips and a short gully as well as a short leg and Greig at silly point. Edmonds bowls again. That was down the leg side ... and he's caught! He's caught at square leg and that is 81 for 5 as they go in to tea. It was Underwood who caught him. He made a pull, didn't quite get hold of it. Underwood leapt for it, caught it. 81 for 5, three wickets to Edmonds in seven balls.

At the other end, Underwood had made run scoring a very rare activity and he also added the wicket of Gilmour for 6 at 96 for 6. But Edmonds was not finished ...

ALAN GIBSON
Let's see what Edmonds can do, as he comes in and bowls ... and he's got him ... caught at first slip! There goes Walker in the fourteenth minute of his innings with the score 104 for 7 not having added, materially, to the total.

ALAN GIBSON
A thin drizzle still falling and the light not very good now. In comes Edmonds and bowls to Walters and Walters tries to heave him round on the leg side, is hit on the pad and he's out, leg before wicket! ... That is Walters, leg before wicket to Edmonds for 19 and Edmonds, in his first Test match, has taken five wickets for 16 runs.

Edmonds finished with five for 28 by the time, on Saturday, when Snow polished off the innings for 135, a deficit of 153. The rest of the day was a tight struggle. Starting their innings an hour into the day's play, England were 184 for 3. The tempo picked up on Monday morning. Greig and Steele took their fourth wicket stand to 94 – Greig making 49 of them. Knott played some splendid improvised shots in his 31 and David Steele was seventh out for 92. England were all out after a hectic morning, 25 minutes before lunch, for 291.

Australia needed 445 in 616 minutes. By the end of the fourth day that apparently impossible target was looking anything but at 220 for 3, despite the loss of both Chappells – Ian for 62 and Greg for 12. McCosker was 95 not out and Walters 25. Speculation and excitement were

AUSTRALIA
FIRST INNINGS
81-5

AUSTRALIA
FIRST INNINGS
104-7

AUSTRALIA
FIRST INNINGS
107-8

Ian Chappell

124

mounting that night at the prospect of a dramatic and maybe historic last day. The day was to be historic, certainly, but in the most anti-climatic way. Overnight, intruders protesting about the imprisonment of George Davis, a Londoner convicted after a bank raid, got under the covers, dug holes and poured oil on the pitch.

66I received the phone call at 8 am. "The pitch has been damaged and the game is in doubt": was the message from the sports room in London.

I must confess my first thoughts ... but I was thinking like a producer at the time ... were: "what the bloody hell are we going to do about the commentary?" And then the sheer enormity of what had happened sank in – a Test match having to be called off because of this sort of publicity-seeking vandalism.

Once at the ground it was a case of lining up the quotes and we recorded just about anyone who had a comment.**99**   **Don Mosey**

TONY GREIG
Oh, I don't think there was any way we could possibly play on that wicket. It's pretty bad and, even forgetting about the oil there's a huge black patch, which would be pretty off-putting. It didn't take us long to agree that there's no way in

125

the world that we could produce anything which was similar to the one we're playing on at the moment. If I could have got Ian Chappell to have played on anything I would have done so.

As it happened there was a further irony. By what would have been the lunch interval the rain was lashing down and the match would not have been finished anyway. With this draw, Australia had retained the Ashes and with another draw at the Oval, they made sure of a series win as well. England had no tour that winter – for the last time until the enforced idleness of 1988/9 – but, to crown the year, David Steele was voted BBC Television's Sports Personality of 1975. He was to play one more Test series, against the West Indies the following summer, but was not picked for the next overseas tour. His moment in the spotlight had passed.

❝The feeling was that this particular danger was past and that now was the time to look for new players. Gooch, having had a traumatic experience in his first Test series in 1975 suddenly started making runs again and, by the 1977 series, was established as the ideal partner for Boycott.❞
Don Mosey

❝Had England been going to Australia or the West Indies that winter instead of India, I think Steele (*right*) would have been around a lot longer. But it was just a glorious romantic episode and a marvellous example of what many county players might do given the chance.❞

Third Test, Headingley, 14-19 August 1975
Match drawn

ENGLAND

J. H. Edrich c Mallett b Thomson	62	b Mallett		35
B. Wood lbw b Gilmour	9	lbw b Walker		25
D. S. Steele c Walters b Thomson	73	c G. Chappell b Gilmour		92
J. H. Hampshire lbw b Gilmour	14	c G. Chappell b Thomson		0
K. W. R. Fletcher c Mallett b Lillee	8	c G. Chappell b Lillee		14
*A. W. Greig run out	51	c & b Mallett		49
†A. P. E. Knott lbw b Gilmour	14	c Thomson b Lillee		31
P. H. Edmonds not out	13	c sub (Turner) b Gilmour		8
C. M. Old b Gilmour	5	st Marsh b Mallett		10
J. A. Snow c Walters b Gilmour	0	c Marsh b Gilmour		9
D. L. Underwood c G. Chappell b Gilmour	0	not out		0
Extras (b4, lb15, w11, nb9)	39	(b5, lb2, w2, nb9)		18
Total	**288**			**291**

AUSTRALIA

R. B. McCosker c Hampshire b Old	0	not out	95
†R. W. Marsh b Snow	25	b Underwood	12
*I. M. Chappell b Edmonds	35	lbw b Old	62
G. S. Chappell c Underwood b Edmonds	13	c Steele b Edmonds	12
R. Edwards lbw b Edmonds	0		
K. D. Walters lbw b Edmonds	19	not out	25
G. J. Gilmour c Greig b Underwood	6		
M. H. N. Walker c Old b Edmonds	0		
J. R. Thomson c Steele b Snow	16		
D. K. Lillee b Snow	11		
A. A. Mallett not out	1		
Extras (lb5, w1, nb3)	9	(b4, lb8, nb2)	14
Total	**135**	(3 wkts)	**220**

BOWLING

AUSTRALIA	O	M	R	W		O	M	R	W
Lillee	28	12	53	1	–	20	5	48	2
Thomson	22	8	53	2	–	20	6	67	1
Gilmour	31.2	10	85	6	–	20	5	72	3
Walker	18	4	54	0	–	15	4	36	1
I. Chappell	2	0	4	0	–				
Mallett					–	19	4	50	3
ENGLAND									
Snow	18.5	7	22	3	–	15	5	21	0
Old	11	3	30	1	–	17	5	61	1
Greig	3	0	14	0	–	9	3	20	0
Wood	5	2	10	0	–				
Underwood	19	12	22	1	–	15	4	40	1
Edmonds	20	7	28	5	–	17	4	64	1

ENGLAND fall of wickets
FIRST INNINGS: 1-25, 2-137, 3-159, 4-189, 5-213, 6-268, 7-269, 8-284, 9-284.
SECOND INNINGS: 1-55, 2-70, 3-103, 4-197, 5-209, 6-210, 7-272, 8-276, 9-285.
AUSTRALIA fall of wickets
FIRST INNINGS: 1-8, 2-53, 3-78, 4-78, 5-81, 6-96, 7-104, 8-107, 9-128.
SECOND INNINGS: 1-55, 2-161, 3-174.

First Test at Edgbaston, July 10-14
Australia won by an innings and 85 runs
Australia 359 (Marsh 61, McCosker 59, Edwards, 56, I. Chappell 52); England 101 (Lillee 5-15, Walker 5-48) and 173 (Fletcher 51, Thomson 5-38).

Second Test at Lord's, July 31-August 5
Match drawn
England 315 (Greig 96, Knott 69, Steele 50) and 436-7 dec (Edrich 175, Wood 52); Australia 268 (Edwards 99, Lillee 73*) and 329-3 (I. Chappell 86, McCosker 79, G. Chappell 73*, Edwards 52*)

Fourth Test at The Oval, August 28-September 3
Match drawn
Australia 532-9 dec (I. Chappell 192, McCosker 127, Walters 65) and 40-2; England 191 and 538 (Woolmer 149, Edrich 96, Roope 77, Steele 66, Knott 64).

AUSTRALIA IN ENGLAND 1977

The Third Test, **Trent Bridge,** *July 28-August 2*
The Fourth Test, **Headingley,** *August 11-15*
Commentators **John Arlott, Brian Johnston, Alan McGilvray,
Christopher Martin-Jenkins and Henry Blofeld**
Summarisers **Trevor Bailey and Fred Trueman**

This was a momentous year for world cricket. In March, the Centenary Test in Melbourne had been a huge success, celebrating one hundred years of Test cricket between England and Australia. Cricket's popularity had aroused the commercial curiosity of the Australian television magnate, Kerry Packer and, in May, news of a revolution which would simply be remembered as "Packer" and which would turn cricket upside down, burst in on an unsuspecting world.

In the long term, the problems caused by the secret defection of 39 of the world's leading players to Packer's proposed televised cricket circus – World Series Cricket – were to disrupt Australian cricket more seriously, but England's captain Tony Greig, at the height of his popularity and success, was found to have been heavily involved in recruiting for Packer and was promptly removed from office.

It was not until July 26 that the International Cricket Conference imposed a deadline of October 1 on anyone contracted to play in the Packer matches to withdraw, or be considered unavailable for Test cricket, and not until November that Mr. Justice Slade, in the High Court, concluded that the ICC's proposed ban represented an unreasonable restraint of trade. The Packer crisis had not yet degenerated into the all-out war it later became, largely because, during the summer of 1977, the world's cricket authorities were still deciding how to react. Therefore, Greig and those Australians who had defected to Packer were still available for the series. Not surprisingly, however, amid claim and counter claim that this or that player had decided to throw in his lot with Packer, it was played out against a dramatic background of uncertainty.

At Lord's the first Test was drawn with honours in the end just about even, thanks to Willis's 9 wickets and Woolmer's century. But at Old Trafford another Woolmer century was rewarded with an England victory as Underwood's 6 second-innings wickets made it a great Kent double.

In 1974 Geoff Boycott had walked out of Test cricket, claiming a need to concentrate on Yorkshire. By 1976 Tony Greig and some of the selectors were making approaches to him to return and in May 1977, Boycott declared his availability again.

He had to wait for a few poor scores from Dennis Amiss in the first two Tests to make a place available. But for the third Test at Trent Bridge he was recalled, and, as he prepared to resume his illustrious career, a 21-year-old Somerset all-rounder had also been called into the England team. His name was Ian Botham.

Both men were to make a significant mark on this match. The Packer affair had just presented them with one of the great captains of Test history, Mike Brearley . . .

Mike Brearley

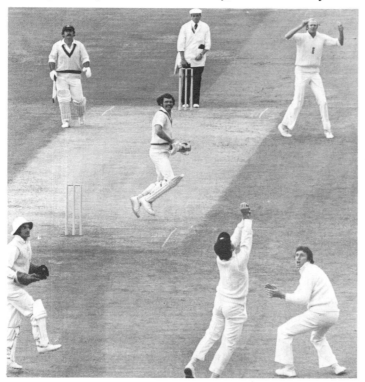

❝I met Brearley when he first went out to South Africa with Mike Smith, having had a marvellous season for Cambridge. A very, very clever chap – no question of that – who regarded cricket as a game of chess in the way it taxed his brain. I don't think he would ever have played as an ordinary player – it wouldn't have demanded enough of him. A very good tactician and a good psychologist. He seemed to give one confidence that things were going to go well – rather like Monty. If you were serving under him, you felt the best was being done for you.

These were Brearley's strengths; an understanding of people and the fact that they would follow him, that he tried for them and he was a good tactician, and came up with a few runs.**❞**

Brian Johnston

Brearley takes a catch off the bowling of Tony Greig, his predecessor as England captain.

129

Greg Chappell won the toss on a glorious morning at Trent Bridge and he had no hesitation in batting and he was at the crease when Australia passed 100 with only one wicket down. Soon after, McCosker fell to Hendrick for 51. But then Brearley made a change in the attack . . .

BRIAN JOHNSTON
So the drinks have come off and Botham has come on instead of Hendrick. Now he runs up and bowls this to Chappell . . . and he's out! He's bowled him! Chappell is out and Botham has got his first Test wicket, and Australia are 131 for 3. The off stump leaning back there, Fred.

FRED TRUEMAN
Well that's a classical case of did the drinks interval break the batsman's concentration? When somebody like Botham comes on, Greg probably thought, "I can relax a little bit here," and he relaxed a little too much, and Botham's got his first Test wicket and he will be very pleased with that.

The wicket of Greg Chappell was a notable first scalp, with over 370 more to come. Willis then had Hookes brilliantly caught at slip by Hendrick with the score 133.

HENRY BLOFELD
Botham has certainly got a cleaner's bill in front of him. He's got a very dirty green left knee. But Botham runs away, he bowls to Walters . . . Walters edges it and he's caught! He's caught by Hendrick in the gully, the finer of the two gullies . . . and that was a most splendid catch. It was low, the ball was travelling fast and he took it very cleanly. So Botham has got another wicket – Walters caught Hendrick bowled Botham for 11, and Australia are now 153 for 5.

ALAN McGILVRAY
I didn't think Botham bowled at all well earlier this morning – 6 overs for 26 runs, but now he's bowling a full length which I heard Trevor and Freddie say that he should. And here is Marsh again . . . and there's an appeal for leg before, and he's out! Botham's third wicket and Marsh out for no score!

ALAN McGILVRAY
Botham's on his way now and Walker is caught at slip! Another catch for Hendrick. Walker out no score . . . caught Hendrick bowled Botham to give Botham his fourth wicket.

AUSTRALIA
FIRST INNINGS
131-3

AUSTRALIA
FIRST INNINGS
153-7

In a spell of 14 balls, Botham had taken 3 wickets for one run and Australia had slumped from 131 for 2 to 155 for 8. The afternoon session had cost them 7 wickets for the addition of 72 runs.

Ian Botham

FRED TRUEMAN

Well, Thomson and O'Keeffe are making the batting that's gone before them look an absolute farce, because they've not looked in trouble at all. They've put on these very valuable 41 runs and it does really make one wonder what happened to Australian middle order batting. It just suddenly folded up like a pack of cards.

HENRY BLOFELD

Botham now starting his 17th over, running away from us. Up, in now to bowl to Thomson, he bowls, Thomson swings and he's caught behind. He slashed at it. Botham has taken his 5th wicket and is getting tremendous congratulations from his team mates. Australia are now 196 for 9.

There was a delay for Her Majesty's visit during her Midland's tour, this came from the last wicket pair, whose stand of 47 she eventually had to interrupt to allow her to continue. When the innings did finish, in the last half hour of the first day, the last two wickets had added 88 and Australia had recovered to 243.

The following morning Len Pascoe removed both Brearley and Woolmer with the score at 34. But that brought in the local Nottingham hero, Derek Randall, playing his first Test on his home ground . . .

JOHN ARLOTT

And the field now – 3 slips and 2 gulleys close to the bat, Thomson comes in, bowls to Boycott, who pushes that . . . there must be a run out here, . . . oh . . . how tragic, how tragic, how tragic. We welcome World Service with the news that Randall has just this minute been sacrificially run out, and England are 52 for 3. Let's leave the applause for Randall from a Trent Bridge crowd as he comes in, very crestfallen and very unlucky. Almost with tears in his eyes, he looks very disconsolate.

Boycott's career was dogged by run-out controversy, but the nature of Randall's untimely dismissal was particularly galling. Boycott was made all too aware of the

ENGLAND
FIRST INNINGS
52-3

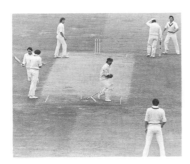

Boycott runs out Randall

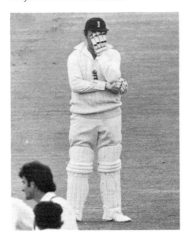

Boycott's despair

hostility of the crowd in this, his first Test innings for three years. He had pushed the ball just past the bowler's stumps and run. With Thomson and particularly Pascoe now giving him a torrid welcome back, Boycott just had to hang on and make the runs that he had denied Randall. Greig went at 64 and Miller at 82, but that brought in just the right man to get Boycott moving again, Alan Knott.

Also, significantly, after a cloudy morning, the sun was coming out and with it England's fortunes rose . . .

BRIAN JOHNSTON
I suppose of all batsmen today Knott has more unorthodox strokes ranging from a 6 over extra-cover, which I've seen him do, to this extraordinary sweep from outside the off-stump, the paddle down to long leg and any sort of improvisation you like, in the way of giving himself room to cut and so on.

TREVOR BAILEY *A very difficult batsman to bowl at.*

BRIAN JOHNSTON
I would think very. And O'Keeffe bowling to him again. He needs one for his 50. Up O'Keeffe comes, and that one he's going to get it, . . . it's gone down to third man. He's cut it down there and that's the hundred partnership as well, and Knott is 50. One of the best I've seen. 184 for 5, Knott 53.
At the end of the second day Boycott and Knott were still there, both in the eighties, with England only one run behind. The crowd on Saturday was huge and ready to forgive Boycott and forget.

HENRY BLOFELD
You can feel the expectancy all round the ground. You can almost hear the proverbial pin drop as Thomson turns and starts in again. Knott on 99, waiting for him . . .
Thomson gets to the crease now, he bowls it, short . . . Knott cuts it . . . there's his 100! Down to third man, Walters fields and the crowd rise all round the boundary boards. Knott takes his cap off, waves his bat and Boycott comes down the wicket to congratulate him, to shake him by the hand. . .

HENRY BLOFELD
Thomson to bowl to Boycott. Will he get his 100? Again this tight atmosphere as Thomson's up to the wicket . . .
he bowls to Boycott, Boycott cuts . . . there it is, I think, down

to third man. Walters is quickly to it, Boycott turns, comes back for the second – he'll have to hurry. He's there! That's his 100, and he raises his hands above his head. Well, what a triumph for Geoffrey Boycott and the spectators all around the ground are rising to him and I don't think anyone here underestimates the measure of what he has achieved.

The pair went on to equal the England sixth wicket record against Australia with a stand of 215 before Boycott was caught at slip off Thomson for 107 and came in to a splendid reception. Just after lunch Thomson also had Knott caught for his highest Test score of 135. Botham made 25 in his first Test innings and England were all out in mid-afternoon for 364 – a lead of 121.

Alan Knott

Though Rick McCosker made a century in the second innings and enjoyed a stand of 94 with David Hookes for the third wicket which took Australia ahead, the target, on a good Trent Bridge pitch, of 189 was not likely to be too much of a problem, especially when Boycott and Brearley had taken their opening stand to 154 on the final afternoon. An element of panic then set in with reports of storms approaching and with Brearley out for 81, two more wickets fell quickly as the batting order was juggled. That just added to the romantic end of this tale of kiss and make up which had Boycott and Randall together at the kill . . .

HENRY BLOFELD

England 186 for 3, just 3 runs needed to win. O'Keeffe bowls to Randall, . . . Randall on drives and I think that's the winning runs! It's going down to the sight screen at the far end, being chased by Pascoe. He stops the ball a yard or two short, but they come back for the third run and Randall has scored the winning run. He is 19 not out and the players come in. 189 for 3, England, and they've won this Third Test Match, by 7 wickets, to go two matches up in the series with just two matches left. Boycott's got his arm round Randall, Randall's laughing, Randall's clapping Boycott, Boycott's raising his bat, both very happy in their different ways.

Knott congratulates Boycott

Boycott's century in that match has been his 98th in first class cricket and, in the days before the fourth Test at Headingley, Yorkshire played Warwickshire at

ENGLAND
SECOND INNINGS
189-3

Randall celebrates

Edgbaston. Boycott made his 99th hundred in the first innings and then, perhaps feeling that a Test on his home ground, rather than a Tuesday in Birmingham would be a better stage for a momentous event, declined to bat in the second innings, even though Yorkshire lost four wickets.

There was a sort of inevitability about what was going to happen, as, after winning the toss, England went past 230 with four wickets down . . .

CHRISTOPHER MARTIN-JENKINS
And it's an awful thing to say, but what's happening at the other end seems almost irrelevant at the moment.

FRED TRUEMAN
Well, yes, the whole interest now for this twenty-two and a half thousand crowd is Geoff Boycott's hundred and nothing else. I reckon that if he gets his hundred now – and he wants four more runs – I reckon this game will be stopped for at least five minutes with the enthusiasm that's going to be shown. You can feel it. I've just been sat outside and you can absolutely feel it. There are people holding their hearts when he plays a shot. The one he hit in the air over there, there was two chaps at the side of me who nearly passed out.

CHRISTOPHER MARTIN-JENKINS
Well, let's hope nobody does because nobody would want to miss it. It's going to be Chappell, then, from the Grandstand End to bowl to Boycott who is hit on the pad here as he aims to play a ball which was floating down the leg side. Thomson comes in from square leg to pick the ball up and the crowd talk amongst themselves with relief. Throats going a little bit dry. People fidgeting in their seats.

Chappell turns, goes in again. Boycott 96 not out. He bowls to him . . . It's a half volley . . . he drives it down the ground . . . and there it is! He's done it! He lifts both hands in the air. Geoff Boycott has got his one hundredth hundred and the crowd cannot resist coming on to the pitch any longer and, Fred, I shall hand straight over to you at this moment of triumph for a very great Yorkshire cricketer.

Peter West, the BBC commentator, shows Boycott the moment of his triumph in action replay

FRED TRUEMAN
He's done it. Fabulous. Great performance. He came here this morning with the intention of getting his head down and getting that hundredth hundred and now he's done it. The

third Yorkshireman, Herbert Sutcliffe, Len Hutton and now Geoff Boycott. Where he is among that lot, I don't know but you can see the enthusiasm and what they think about him up here in this county.

Boycott, 110 not out overnight, very nearly gave the second day crowd a double century to celebrate when he was last out for 191. He had again enjoyed his best partnership for the sixth wicket with Knott, who made 57 out of 123.

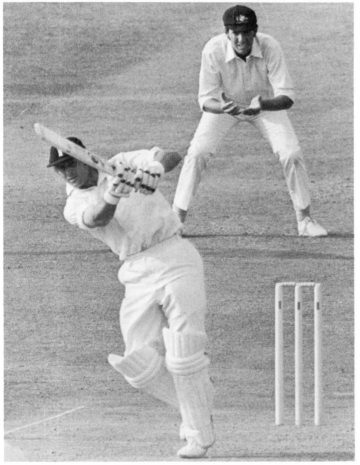

Facing an England score of 436, Australia were immediately in trouble on the Friday evening and Hendrick and Botham completed the demolition on Saturday morning with 4 and 5 wickets respectively to dismiss them for 103. Following on, there was rather more resistance. For Australia, the possibility of saving the match was

❝Boycott was a very strange person, but, well-handled, he was very different and the chap who had handled him marvellously was Mike Smith on the 1965/66 tour of Australia. He jokingly called him 'Fiery' which Boycs rather liked. He was clearly a manufactured player. He learnt it all out of text books. There it was – a textbook playing cricket and all learnt by watching and being coached and practice, practice, practice.
I said to him, "You know I don't consider you a complete batsman because you don't take an attack by storm". And he said, "Well, no. You see I am the best batsman in the side and so I must not take the risks. The others must." He was quite straightforward about it.
I asked about the run outs and he said, "I mustn't be the one run out. The other people have got to make the sacrifices." He quite genuinely believed it.
He would have made the best professional golfer there's ever been. He could have played for himself and not run anyone out.**❞**
Brian Johnston

Boycott scores the boundary which brings up his 100th hundred.

enhanced by the loss of most of the fourth day's play to the weather. But then, on the last day there was no escape…

CHRISTOPHER MARTIN-JENKINS

It will be Marsh to face and Hendrick to bowl, with the attacking field loosened slightly for the left-hander and the well-set batsman … Four slips – and here's Hendrick again, running in to bowl to Marsh, 63 not out. Marsh swings it high on the off side – Randall's underneath it – this could be the Ashes for England … He's caught it – they've won! The Ashes for England! Randall turns a cartwheel – the stumps are seized by the players – the crowd come on to the field and England have regained the Ashes.

A really wonderful moment for Mike Brearley, for Hendrick who took the wicket, for all the England side who outplayed Australia. And now a kaleidoscope of small figures sprinting towards the pavilion – Randall taking the catch and somehow that was the most ideal ending, I think really, with this exuberant character, who is destined to become one of the great characters of cricket in the years ahead, I'm sure; who had an unforgettable innings at Melbourne which heralded better things for England and now they have happened.

So, at twenty to five – 4.39, to be precise – England have bowled Australia out for 248. They've won by an innings and 85 runs. Hendrick has taken the final wicket, but the honours have been unquestionably shared by all those concerned.

TREVOR BAILEY

Well, Marsh – in an impossible position – went for the big one and Randall doesn't drop catches – not like that – caught it joyfully. And England have won. I don't think anyone would deny that they have been consistently the better side throughout this series and, in this particular match, they have fielded a lot better, they have bowled a lot better and they have batted a lot better. The victory, of course, was basically set up by Boycott; Boycott, who scored 190 odd runs, which really set the whole scene. Without Boycott's innings it would have been a much closer game of cricket. I think, probably, England would still have won, but he set it all up and then the England seam bowlers, Hendrick in particular, bowled considerably better than the Australian seamers, because largely he bowled at the wicket and he moved the ball.

Randall's joy

Third Test, Trent Bridge, 28 July-2 August 1977
England won by 7 wickets

AUSTRALIA

R. B. McCosker c Brearley b Hendrick	51	c Brearley b Willis	107
I. C. Davis c Botham b Underwood	33	c Greig b Willis	9
*G. S. Chappell b Botham	19	b Hendrick	27
D. W. Hookes c Hendrick b Willis	17	lbw b Hendrick	42
K. D. Walters c Hendrick b Botham	11	c Randall b Greig	28
R. D. Robinson c Brearley b Greig	11	lbw b Underwood	34
†R. W. Marsh lbw b Botham	0	c Greig b Willis	0
K. J. O'Keeffe not out	48	not out	21
M. H. N. Walker c Hendrick b Botham	0	b Willis	17
J. R. Thomson c Knott b Botham	21	b Willis	0
L. S. Pascoe c Greig b Hendrick	20	c Hendrick b Underwood	0
Extras (b4, lb2, nb6)	12	(b1, lb5, w1, nb17)	24
Total	**243**		**309**

ENGLAND

*J. M. Brearley c Hookes b Pascoe	15	b Walker	81
G. Boycott c McCosker b Thomson	107	not out	80
R. A. Woolmer lbw b Pascoe	0		
D. W. Randall run out	13	not out	19
A. W. Greig b Thomson	11	b Walker	0
G. Miller c Robinson b Pascoe	13		
†A. P. E. Knott c Davis b Thomson	135	c O'Keeffe b Walker	2
I. T. Botham b Walker	25		
D. L. Underwood b Pascoe	7		
M. Hendrick b Walker	1		
R. G. D. Willis not out	2		
Extras (b9, lb7, w3, nb16)	35	(b2, lb2, w1, nb2)	7
Total	**364**	(3 wkts dec.)	**189**

BOWLING								
ENGLAND	O	M	R	W	O	M	R	W
Willis	15	0	58	1	26	6	88	5
Hendrick	21.2	6	46	2	32	14	56	2
Botham	20	5	74	5	25	5	60	0
Greig	15	4	35	1	9	2	24	1
Underwood	11	5	18	1	27	15	49	2
Miller					5	2	5	0
Woolmer					3	0	3	0
AUSTRALIA								
Thomson	31	6	103	3	16	6	34	0
Pascoe	32	10	80	4	22	6	43	0
Walker	39.2	12	79	2	24	8	40	3
Chappell	8	0	19	0				
O'Keeffe	11	4	43	0	19.2	2	65	0
Walters	3	0	5	0				

AUSTRALIA fall of wickets
FIRST INNINGS: 1-79, 2-101, 3-131, 4-133, 5-153, 6-153, 7-153, 8-155, 9-196.
SECOND INNINGS: 1-18, 2-60, 3-154, 4-204, 5-240, 6-240, 7-270, 8-307, 9-308.
ENGLAND fall of wickets
FIRST INNINGS: 1-34, 2-34, 3-52, 4-65, 5-82, 6-297, 7-326, 8-357, 9-357.
SECOND INNINGS: 1-154, 2-156, 3-158.

First Test at Lord's, June 16-21
Match drawn
England 216 (Woolmer 79, Randall 53)
and 305 (Woolmer 120, Greig 91);
Australia 296 (Serjeant 81, G. Chappell
66, Walters 53, Willis 7-78) and 114-6
(Hookes 50).

Second Test at Old Trafford, July 7-12
England won by 9 wickets
Australia 297 (Walters 88) and 218
(G. Chappell 112, Underwood 6-66);
England 437 (Woolmer 137, Randall 79,
Greig 76) and 82-1.

Fourth Test at Headingley, August 11-15
England won by an innings and 185 runs
England 436 (Boycott 191, Knott 57);
Australia 103 (Botham 5-21) and 248
(Marsh 63).

Fifth Test at The Oval, August 25-30
Match drawn
England 214 (Malone 5-63) and 57-2;
Australia 385 (Hookes 85, Walker 78*,
Marsh 57, Willis 5-102).

AUSTRALIA IN ENGLAND 1981

The Third Test, **Headingley,** *July 16-21*
The Fourth Test, **Edgbaston,** *July 30-August 2*
The Fifth Test, **Old Trafford,** *August 13-17*
Commentators **Brian Johnston, Henry Blofeld, Alan McGilvray,
Christopher Martin-Jenkins and Don Mosey**
Summarisers **Trevor Bailey and Fred Trueman**

All the things that every schoolboy cricketer dreams
came true for Ian Botham in the incredible tests of
1981, and the sporting mood of a nation was
transformed from desperation to delirium by his, and
England's extraordinary feats. For one man, however,
there was an added degree of poignancy in the
unfolding of the drama which made this series one of
the most memorable in cricket history.

❝I really did retire one series too
early. I would love to have been
able to commentate on that 1981
series.**❞**   **John Arlott**

Although it was a glorious season – for Englishmen, at
least, it had inauspicious beginnings. England had lost in
the West Indies at home in 1980 and away the following
winter. Ian Botham was the defeated captain, in both
instances, not enjoying the best personal form. He held on
to the job for the start of the Ashes series and at Trent
Bridge scored four runs and took three wickets as Lillee
and Alderman put Australia one up. At Lord's, despite a
draw, it was worse for Botham.

66 The atmosphere was electric. To me, Botham had demonstrated in West Indies, beyond all shadow of doubt, that the captaincy had affected his play. It was inevitable that the job would have to be taken away from him. The selectors just needed a peg to hang it on. When he bagged a pair at Lord's that was the peg and he forestalled them by a minute by resigning just as Alec Bedser was about to sack him.

Having to lead by example only put a lot of pressure on Botham to perform. If his great worth was leading by example, the example had to be produced all the time. Mike Brearley had been sounded out. He didn't want to tour again but was prepared to captain at home, I think partly in the hope that he could restore Botham because he had a genuine regard and affection for him. It might have been that, having nominated Botham to the selectors in the first place, he wanted to see his judgment justified.

The feeling was we were just second best and nothing that happened on the first three days at Headingley did anything to change our view of that. The performance was abject. **99**   **Don Mosey**

With Brearley installed as captain, Botham kept his place for Headingley, despite his recent form. Another key figure in the drama which was to unfold very nearly did not. Bob Willis had to convince the selectors, who had not intended to include him, that he was fit enough to play.

Australia won the toss and between them John Dyson and Graeme Wood put on 55 against the England seam attack of Willis, Old and Dilley. Brearley turned to the erstwhile golden arm ...

DON MOSEY
Now it is Botham from the Kirkstall Lane end and it is a very good one, there is an appeal, and he is out. That came back and beat Wood on the back defensive stroke and Ian Botham strikes straight away, third ball of his first spell of this game. Wood lbw bowled Botham for 34. Australia are 55 for 1.

AUSTRALIA
FIRST INNINGS
55-1

139

Dennis Lillee

ENGLAND
FIRST INNINGS
144-6

ENGLAND
FIRST INNINGS
162-7

ENGLAND
SECOND INNINGS
0-1

Botham, as if to celebrate the casting off of the shackles of captaincy, was to finish with six wickets for 95, but by then Australia had made tremendous strides towards winning the match by making 401 for 9, by the time Kim Hughes declared, late on the second day. Dyson had made a determined 102, Hughes 89 and Graham Yallop 58 and this, on an apparently unreliable pitch. It certainly looked that way when England batted on it. Alderman had Gooch at 12 and Brearley at 40 and Lawson removed Boycott at 43 and Gower at 84. When Lillee had Gatting lbw, England were deep in the mire at 87 for 5. But coming in at number seven was Ian Botham …

ALAN McGILVRAY
Next ball from Alderman to Botham. What will he do?
He dips in to it, drives a beautiful shot for 4 runs, straight down past mid off. He timed that beautifully and sent it on its way. How many 4's is that Bill? His eighth. Eight 4's in 41 balls and he is 46. Well, he is heading for the "man-of-the-match" if he keeps going like this, isn't he?

HENRY BLOFELD
It is Alderman again, off his short run. In, bowls to Botham. Botham carves this away square on the off side. Yallop, down at square third man fields, and that is Ian Botham's 50. The crowds' hands are clapping all around the ground, flags are waving, Union Jacks, Cornhill flags, tremendous jubilation and how pleased and happy Ian Botham must feel, 6 for 95 and now a magnificent typical Botham 50.

He got no further than that – his dismissal off Lillee giving Rod Marsh the world record number of test wicket-keeping victims. The record of 263 was held by Alan Knott until this dismissal.

By the end of the third day, England were following on, 226 behind – all out for 174. That was not the end of an awful Saturday for them …

DON MOSEY
Lillee in, from the Kirkstall Lane end, bowling to Gooch. And Gooch gets an edge and he is caught, he is caught! It is Alderman at third slip, he was immediately engulfed by colleagues. England have lost their first second innings wicket to the third ball of the innings, Gooch, caught

Alderman bowled Lillee, no score. England, following on 227 runs behind, are none for one.

At the close of the third day, England needed another 215 from their last nine wickets to make Australia bat again. The most humiliating odds flashed up on the huge electronic scoreboard, 500-1 *against* an England win. Nobody at the time thought that to be at all unreasonable, though Dennis Lillee and Rod Marsh felt it would be prudent not to ignore such a gamble.

Most of the team and attendant press had booked out of their hotels on the Monday morning – a perfectly sensible move, following the steady procession of England batsmen back into the pavilion.

It was 18 for 2 when Brearley went, 37 for 3 at the fall of Gower's wicket and 41 for 4 at Gatting's dismissal. Peter Willey joined Geoff Boycott in a fifth wicket stand of 64, but Willey went at 105 and Boycott at 133. Botham was joined by Bob Taylor …

ENGLAND
SECOND INNINGS
135-7

DON MOSEY
England, now 92 runs away from making Australia bat again as Taylor faces Alderman. He bowls … and Taylor is caught off bat and pad at short leg, unable to fend off a ball which lifted round to the rib area. Taylor is caught Bright, bowled Alderman 1 and England are 135 for 7.

TREVOR BAILEY *I think the writing is on the wall.*

The last three wickets had to raise another 98 runs just to avoid an innings defeat. Graham Dilley had come in to join Botham …

HENRY BLOFELD
Although we are in the dying moments of the match, England 170 for 7, still 57 runs behind, we are seeing some attractive cricket. Both Botham, who is 34 and Dilley, who is 24, are putting bat to ball and runs are coming at quite a speed and in very entertaining fashion…

Lillee in, bowling now to Botham, outside the off stump … he hammers this, square through the covers. A lovely, forcing shot off the back foot between Chappell at cover point and Bright at extra.

ENGLAND
SECOND INNINGS
228-7

FRED TRUEMAN *Australia have got to bat again.*

HENRY BLOFELD *They have indeed. They are 1 in the lead.*

66I suppose while Dilley (*right*) was in one just had a slight flicker of what could just happen, but one didn't believe it.**99**   <u>Henry Blofeld</u>

66As far as I'm concerned it was all due to Dilley. He seemed to inspire in Botham a kind of perverse attacking courage. He could not have thought it could continue. A few blows coming off is one thing but if it keeps coming off then the mood changes … and that is exactly what happened.

At first Botham (*right*) was playing in a kind of nondescript way as though defeat was inevitable. After all they must have thought it was. But then Dilley started stroking it around and I could see Botham catching on. I could actually see the thoughts going through Botham's mind … "Who does Dilley think he is … I'm the all-rounder" … And of course then, everything he tried came off — slices, edges, one six over third man and on and on.**99** <u>Don Mosey</u>

FRED TRUEMAN
The Australian bowlers who have been in command for so long — suddenly, they do not really know where to bowl because the stick is being dished out. They are bowling a little bit wide and giving Dilley a lot of room and he is liking that. With the room he is getting, it is giving him chance to swing that bat and when he middles it, doesn't it go?

HENRY BLOFELD
Lillee in again, bowls to Dilley, Dilley carves this away ... 4 runs! That was a magnificent stroke, he hit it away, it is his 50, through the covers, through extra, on the up. Botham shakes him by the hand, Dilley acknowledges the applause of the crowd with his bat, and the score goes on to 243 for 7 and two or three of the England players have come out on to the balcony and are applauding Graham Dilley.

ENGLAND
SECOND INNINGS
243-7

66 You could watch through the Monday, first of all doubts beginning to seep into the minds of the Australians, then a lack of faith in themselves and Kim Hughes without the strength of character to control the situation. Morale oozed away. The more Botham carved away the more it came off and the Aussies, Lawson in particular, lost their nerve. Lawson, quite ostentatiously, lost his temper bowling a beamer and a lot of associated rubbish.

The more the situation deteriorated for Australia the more ebullient Botham became and it was the most exhilarating time to be commentating. Even if we had lost still we had had this dash of heroics the like of which we had never seen. 99 **Don Mosey**

ALAN McGILVRAY
Can he get this one run? It is Lawson running in and bowling to him, Botham swings it, it is 4 runs, it is 4 more and it's his 100!

TREVOR BAILEY
Well, it was a magnificent century. It came quickly, it came in most spectacular fashion. It contained some wonderful shots. We shan't see a better 100 this season.

ENGLAND
SECOND INNINGS
288-8

143

66 When Botham was playing that incredible innings, one felt that it was faint but pursuing. The position was so desperate. It was a lot of fun and worth giving a good cheer, but it was just delaying the inevitable. 99 **Henry Blofeld**

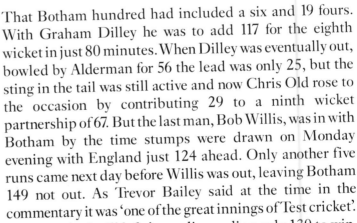

That Botham hundred had included a six and 19 fours. With Graham Dilley he was to add 117 for the eighth wicket in just 80 minutes. When Dilley was eventually out, bowled by Alderman for 56 the lead was only 25, but the sting in the tail was still active and now Chris Old rose to the occasion by contributing 29 to a ninth wicket partnership of 67. But the last man, Bob Willis, was in with Botham by the time stumps were drawn on Monday evening with England just 124 ahead. Only another five runs came next day before Willis was out, leaving Botham 149 not out. As Trevor Bailey said at the time in the commentary it was 'one of the great innings of Test cricket'.

But it had still left Australia needing only 130 to win. Surely that was not enough of a target. By this time, it seemed inevitable that Ian Botham, bowling down the hill, should get an early wicket and he obliged by having Wood caught behind at 13. Bob Willis, meanwhile, had been bowling up the Headingley slope. He protested to Brearley and was granted a change of end.

ALAN McGILVRAY

Willis, from the far end of the ground to Trevor Chappell ... who gets a nasty one on the shoulder ... he is out! It must have run off the glove and then up on to the shoulder and Taylor moved in underneath it and Chappell is out. He tried to take his bat away but it must have hit the glove or the handle.

It skied up, anyhow, and so Chappell is out for 8, caught Taylor bowled Willis and it is 56 for 2 . . .

HENRY BLOFELD
Willis is almost with us, bowling the first ball of the new over from the Kirkstall Lane end. Up now, he bowls to Hughes. Hughes goes back — he is out! He is caught! He is caught by Botham at third slip, low to his left and Australia have lost their third wicket for 58! Hughes is out for a duck, caught Botham bowled Willis for 0 and that is the wicket England badly wanted just before lunch . . .

Fifty-eight for 3, Australia needing 130 to win. They want 72 more runs and this game is by no means over! A tight, attacking field and here is Willis again, bowling for his life, bowls now to Yallop . . . bowls and . . . he is out! He is caught at forward short leg — he is caught by Gatting. It lifted on him, he played it, could not keep it down, Gatting came forward, got both hands to it, threw it in the air and Australia go in to lunch 58 for 4. Yallop caught Gatting bowled Willis for 0. Well, Fred what an over!

FRED TRUEMAN *What an over, what a transformation!*

Soon after lunch, two more wickets fell at 65 and 68. The tension was mounting, not just among those at the ground, but in cars on the country's motorways, in offices and homes and even on one express train out of Paddington, whose guard announced each wicket over the public address as it fell.

AUSTRALIA
SECOND INNINGS
56-2

AUSTRALIA
SECOND INNINGS
58-3

AUSTRALIA
SECOND INNINGS
58-4

66It was a performance geared to the atmosphere of the game, he plugged into the charge.

It is fiendishly difficult for Bob (*left*) with his ungainly action to bowl down that slope at Headingley. Everything was against him but you could see the players geeing him up and the Aussies' morale just went, their bottle completely disappeared and they played shots they will be ashamed of for the rest of their lives. They were shell-shocked by a performance so incredible that they must never have considered they would experience the like.99
Don Mosey

66One of the distortions of that match is that it is remembered as Botham's match — which it was — but you must never forget Willis's wickets.99   **Henry Blofeld**

145

**AUSTRALIA
SECOND INNINGS
74-7**

❝ Not until Dilley took that skier from Marsh, with his heels practically on the boundary rope did I really feel that England would win. **❞** **Henry Blofeld**

❝ Brearley's coolness was splendid as the runs mounted and Australia got past 100. That must surely have been his finest hour as a captain. There was not the slightest panic. He was always totally in control. **❞** **Henry Blofeld**

DON MOSEY
Willis in, bowling now to the left-handed Marsh who tries to swing him away ... it is high in the air and underneath it is Dilley — and Dilley catches it just inside the boundary. He did a quick step to make sure he was inside the ropes and Australia are 74 for 7. They still need 56 to win, England need now only three wickets.

DON MOSEY
Willis bowls to Lawson, who edges it — and he is caught by Taylor! And that's a world record number of catches for Bob Taylor ... Australia are 75 for 8.

Ray Bright was now joined by Dennis Lillee, and they began to claw Australia back into the game. They posted their side's hundred and English onlookers began again to feel the certainty of defeat creeping up on them.

Mike Brearley and Bob Willis

HENRY BLOFELD

And here he comes, shoulders forward, accelerating up to the wicket in a sprint now. He bowls to Lillee, Lillee steps away, cuts ... 4 runs. It goes into the boundary and another 4 to Dennis Lillee, a perfectly good square cut. Australia 110 for 8. These two have now put on 35 runs, Lillee goes to 17, Bright is 19 and Australia need 20 runs to win. And here comes Willis, in, bowls to Lillee, Lillee hits this, he is going to be caught! I think ... no ... yes — he is caught by Gatting at mid on! He chipped that one up, Gatting ran in and caught it low down on the ground as he fell forward. They all go round Gatting, Bob Taylor comes jumping in to congratulate him. Lillee is out, caught Gatting bowled Willis for 17, Australia are 110 for 9 and Willis has now taken seven wickets.

TREVOR BAILEY

Most of the Australian side inside the dressing room, cannot watch.

HENRY BLOFELD

Willis to Bright, Bright is 19, Australia 111 for 9, 19 short of victory. Here is Willis, in, bowls to Bright ... Bright bowled! The middle stump is out of the ground, England have won! They have won by 18 runs! Willis runs around punching the air, the boys invade the ground and the players run helter-skelter for the pavilion. Well, what a finish, Bright bowled Willis for 19, Willis has taken eight wickets for 43 — the best ever by an English bowler here at Headingley against Australia, a phenomenal performance by Bob Willis and Australia all out for 111. England have won by 18 runs.

**AUSTRALIA
SECOND INNINGS
110-9**

Ray Bright is bowled by Willis – an unforgettable sight for England

❝It just couldn't happen. But it did. It was the most historic occasion and yet it wasn't a real cricket occasion. It was a fluke, a massive, incredible fluke.**❞**
Don Mosey

Terry Alderman

Nine days later, with the series now all square, the Fourth Test started at Edgbaston. Brearley won the toss and chose to bat on what looked a splendid batting pitch. He would have been amazed to know then that by the time the match finished – a day early – no batsman would reach fifty. On that first day, Alderman led the way taking 5 for 42 in the rout of England for 189. But it was not entirely Australia's day. Before the close, Chris Old had reduced them to 19 for 2. The next day, Kim Hughes and the new cap, Martin Kent, were at the centre of an Australian recovery which helped them into the lead with only five wickets down. After that, they must have been disappointed with the eventual lead of just 69.

It looked a useful enough lead, though, when England were 115 for 6 with the slow left armer, Ray Bright, having taken five of them. Emburey led some resistance in his own, idiosyncratic style to get the total up to 219 on the third evening, but Australia's target was only 151. Even after the loss of Wood before the close, that looked a formality.

On that fourth day, a Sunday, Willis had Dyson lbw at 19 and then tempted Hughes to hook one to square leg and the score was 29 for 3. Thoughts of Headingley must have been flitting through Australian minds. But a former and a future Australian captain came together to restore the balance in their favour. The runs began to flow for Allan Border and Graham Yallop. Only 64 runs were needed, with seven wickets in hand …

 CHRISTOPHER MARTIN-JENKINS
Emburey still has three men round the bat on the off side, and one forward short leg — and it's Yallop to face. He's 30 not out. Emburey asking Boycott at mid-on to go a little bit wider. Now he comes in, round the wicket, to bowl to Yallop … Oh and he's caught by Ian Botham! He went to hit the ball away on the on side, got an outside edge and the ball carried to Botham. Emburey has got the break-through for England and Yallop's patchy innings is over. A very valuable one in the circumstances for Australia, and he may well have stayed there long enough to frustrate England. On the other hand, there is still some way for Australia to go. It's 87 for 4.

AUSTRALIA
SECOND INNINGS
87-4

ALAN McGILVRAY

He's certainly batting very well, but he's getting some troubles from this man Emburey, and who wouldn't? The score now 105. Forty-six wanted by Australia, or six wickets to England. And it's Border again and it's a nasty one ... there's an appeal for a catch — and he's caught! That one lifted and hit the bat and it flicked away out to short square leg, where Gatting is fielding and Border is out for 40.

Kent and Marsh were together now and the score continued to nudge up towards the inevitable if not quite comfortable Australian victory. As a last, desperate throw, Brearley called on a reluctant Ian Botham to bowl.

AUSTRALIA
SECOND INNINGS
105-5

BRIAN JOHNSTON
Marsh just pushes his helmet firmer down. I wouldn't have thought he needed a helmet today, but I think they get into the habit of wearing them. And here's Botham coming in, bowls this one ... That's bowled him! Middle stump knocked out of the ground. Marsh is bowled Botham for 4. The match is swinging England's way again and Australia are 114 for 6 with the batsmen to come in, Bright, Lillee, Alderman, Hogg. So, Marsh comes back and now we have Bright. Bright, who made 27 in the first innings. Yes, a ball very well pitched up to Marsh and the middle stump bowling out of the ground! A marvellous sight for a bowler but a bit depressing for the batsman. I wouldn't like to bet on this at all. It really is terrifyingly exciting ... 37 runs needed, four wickets to fall!

TREVOR BAILEY *Oh dear, oh dear!*

BRIAN JOHNSTON
And you couldn't believe this could happen again. This is Headingley again and it's marvellous! We had some rather mediocre play on the first three days and then suddenly the fourth day produces this magnificent cricket! Now, Botham to bowl to Bright. Two slips, third man, backward point, cover, mid off, mid on, square leg and a long leg. And here is Botham coming in. He's getting the Willis cheer now as he comes in — Bowls that — its hit him on the pad ... He's out! — Out first ball! Bright lbw Botham 0, and it looked plumbers from here. . .

AUSTRALIA
SECOND INNINGS
114-7

TONY LEWIS
120 for 7, 151 required for victory. Three wickets England require for victory. Botham bowls to Lillee. Oh, wide ... he slashes — appeal for a catch behind the wicket! Everyone goes up! — The umpire's hand goes up and Lillee goes! A wonderful catch by Bob Taylor.

AUSTRALIA
SECOND INNINGS
120-8

FRED TRUEMAN
What I like about it was that the umpire, Don Oslear, he thought about it. He took the picture back through his mind and then he gave him out, caught behind the wicket and I don't think there's anything wrong with an umpire that thinks about the situation and relives it before he gives a decision.

CHRISTOPHER MARTIN-JENKINS
Botham bounces in from the far end. He's got his old bounce back too. And he bowls — hits the pad ... an

*appeal for lbw! Not out says umpire Oslear. But thousands of
hearts in mouths again for that split second before umpire
Oslear shook his head. Thirty runs to win, two wickets to fall
and anything but a breathless hush in the close tonight, more
like a breathful roar. Quarter of an hour to tea unless the ninth
wicket falls. Up comes Botham. Bowls and — bowls him!
Bowls him off his pads. Bit unlucky, Kent but the ninth wicket
has gone down and England are on the verge of a second
successive sensational victory. The crowd stand. Their arms in
the air waving away as if it's royal wedding day all over again,
and the dark figure of Martin Kent walks out, head bowed,
towards the sanctuary of the pavilion which will seem a rather
melancholy place to him. 121 for 9. One wicket to fall, 30 still
needed.*

AUSTRALIA
SECOND INNINGS
121-9

CHRISTOPHER MARTIN-JENKINS
*What a marvellous performance it has been by Mike
Brearley and the England team again. Brearley, in these
circumstances, as a captain, is really marvellous at keeping the
pressure on the batsman.*

FRED TRUEMAN
*I'd persuade him to play for the next 10 years, if I were
the selectors.*

CHRISTOPHER MARTIN-JENKINS
*They all seem to bowl for him too don't they? Up comes
Botham now. He bowls to Alderman — and he bowls
him! And England have won! 121 all out Australia, England
have won by 29 runs.*

*And the stumps are uprooted by the players as souvenirs.
The disconsolate figure of Rodney Hogg is lost amongst the sea
of spectators as he is the last player to leave the field. A
tired-looking Dickie Bird is behind him and the spectators
come on like ants round a tasty bit of meat. An incredible spell
by Ian Botham has finished off Australia. Fourteen overs, 9
maidens, 5 for 11. Australia have been beaten by 29 runs and
England go 2-1 up in this series. I think the Australians are
marvellous in defeat and I see Phil Ridings there, the
Chairman of their selectors and the Chairman of their Board.
I feel sorry for him and all Australians at this moment but the
fact is that it's been a great performance by England. England's
bowlers, the bowlers we were deriding only a few weeks ago!*

AUSTRALIA
SECOND INNINGS
121 all out

❝There was no reason at all for it to have happened but I think they were still absolutely shell shocked from his batting performance at Headingley. I could see their minds working "What can this bastard pull off now? The ball is moving both ways, swinging in the air as well and fizzing like a rocket off the pitch. We've had it". They were demoralised.**❞**   **Don Mosey**

Botham bowls Alderman to give England a 2-1 lead in the series

In his last 28 balls in the match, Botham had taken 5 wickets for 1 run and Australia had lost their last six wickets for just 16. The following week, they were to face these same English Houdinis at Old Trafford. With Lawson having missed the Edgbaston Test, Australia now found themselves struggling for a third seam bowler and when Hogg was declared unfit, Mike Whitney, a left arm fast-medium bowler with Gloucestershire, was called in for what would be only his seventh first-class game.

England won the toss and made 231. After being 109 for 6 and 137 for 8, that represented quite a recovery largely due to Chris Tavaré's limpet-like qualities, making 69, and some thrilling tail-end batting by England's Test debutant, Paul Allott. He made 52 not out, sharing a stand of 56 for the last wicket with Bob Willis. Despite a desperate looking assault by Graeme Wood, Willis and Allott tore into the Australians with the ball. Willis started it in his third over, in which he took three wickets. Allott immediately sent back Wood and Australia were 24 for 4. Despite Martin Kent's 52, the slide had started and they were rapidly all out for 130. They were to be given just one further glimpse of a possible escape – so typical of this tantalising series – when on Saturday England's fifth wicket was down for 104 and Tavaré was grinding along at snail's pace. But then in came Ian Botham...

 HENRY BLOFELD
Lillee now in to Botham. He bowls. It's short, Botham hooks. This is in the air. It's going for 6! It goes into the crowd at deep backward square leg for 6. Well, Lillee bowled Botham the bait. Botham took it, and won! He hit it beautifully and it went far into the crowd over there by the scoreboard at deep backward square leg for 6. Forty-one now to Ian Botham, 163 for 5 the score and that was a marvellous piece of challenging, competitive cricket. Lillee v Botham. And the vibrancy has, all of a sudden, returned to Old Trafford and a nice gesture out there Botham and Lillee exchange a laugh.

 FRED TRUEMAN
Actually Dennis Lillee clapped him when he hit the six, did you see that?

ENGLAND
SECOND INNINGS
163-5

153

Dennis Lillee

**ENGLAND
SECOND INNINGS
177-5**

HENRY BLOFELD
Sixty-two to Tavaré, 167 for 3 and, as so often happens, a batsman who seems to have fallen asleep suddenly has a partner who hits the ball, and the spirit of rejuvenation communicates itself. Tavaré is playing his strokes too. Lillee bowls again. It's a short one – Botham hooks and Whitney goes round ... It's six more! It's six more at long leg! Another magnificent stroke! It was short, Botham was quickly inside the line, hit it beautifully. Whitney set off round the fine leg boundary but that was over the top into the crowd and, really, Bobby Charlton might well have scored a goal up the road at Old Trafford, such is the jubilation of the spectators over there in front of the scoreboard. 173 for 5. Ian Botham 48 and what a phenomenal cricketer this man Botham is! Sixteen off the over in four balls. Here's Lillee again, what's it to be this time? In, he bowls. Botham carves at this. There's going to be four more. It is! It's gone square of the wicket for four runs. It was short, but not as short as all that. The momentum is tremendous. It's his fifty. He carved it away – no-one moved – four runs. Fifty-two now to Botham, 177 for 5 the score and this is a different ball game to that which was being played this morning and in the first hour of the afternoon. Everyone, all round the ground cheering, waving flags, recognising that a national hero is doing his stuff again. Sixty balls, 2 sixes and 6 fours! Fred what's happening, you're laughing!

FRED TRUEMAN
I've never seen anything like it. You know, we were watching a wake about two and a half hours ago and now everything's happening ...

HENRY BLOFELD
Botham, needing six more runs for his second hundred of the series and an innings as incredible as that one at Headingley. It seems almost unfair that a normal mortal should play such an innings twice in a series.
Here's Bright to Botham needing six for his hundred. Botham sweeps and is going to get one maybe two. Lillee has a bit of a chase. He's going to get there. He does, throws back to Marsh and Botham is off the mark, underway again after tea with 2 runs. He goes to 96 needing just four more now for that hundred and 228 for 5 is the score. Bright walks back to his

mark at the far end. David Constant scratches his left ear and here comes Bright, over the wicket in, bowls to Botham – Botham swings again, hits that – It's in the air ... Lillee's underneath it ... It's six runs! It's six runs! That's his hundred. Lillee was near it. He jumped for it. He couldn't get to it, and Botham has swept Bright for six! He has 102 out of 234 for 5 and a boy in jeans and black sweater comes on, embraces Botham, kisses him, pats him on the back and then runs back to the crowd from whence he came.

 BILL FRINDALL
His hundred took just 86 balls and that's one fewer than he took to reach his hundred at Headingley.

ENGLAND
SECOND INNINGS
234-5

 FRED TRUEMAN
It's not slogging. It's beautiful clean hitting and the two fours he hit in the last over – I defy anybody to have stopped them.

 BRIAN JOHNSTON
They were marvellous. Well here is Whitney coming up to bowl to him now and he ... caught at the wicket ... He was trying to steer it down to third man, got a top edge, taken by Marsh and a great innings has come to an end. The whole of Old Trafford is already standing up and cheering and Botham is caught Marsh, bowled Whitney for 118 magnificent runs. England are 253 for 6. I think we should keep quiet and just listen to the crowd cheering this tremendous innings. (applause) And really what more can be said! That tells it all, and he looked back at the crowd as he walked in as if to say thanks very much, but I've enjoyed it as much as you did.

Botham hooks Lillee for six

155

ENGLAND
SECOND INNINGS
253-6

66 It was a cultured, magnificent display of power hitting. Australia had pulled themselves back with a few wickets and then this pulverising innings from Botham (*right*) came along and if ever a side were going to be demoralised by an innings, that was it. **99**

Henry Blofeld

FRED TRUEMAN
I feel sure that everybody on this ground – and it's packed – will be talking about this century for years to come and saying the usual thing 'I was there.' Well there'll be twenty odd thousand people can quite rightly say that.

Botham and Tavaré had added 149 for the sixth wicket and Tavaré had made 28 of them. He was eventually Alderman's fifth victim for 78, but there were more runs to come for England in the shape of half centuries from Knott and Emburey. The fact that the last four wickets were able to add over 150 runs proved vital. England were eventually out for 404, setting Australia 506 to win.

With plenty of time in hand, there were times when it seemed just possible – and wholly in keeping with this extraordinary series – that they would get there. Border and Yallop both got to three figures and Australia finished with their second-highest total for the fourth innings of a Test Match. But it was all in vain...

BRIAN JOHNSTON
We have five slips and a point very close in. Everybody hovering round poor Whitney, as Bob Willis comes in and bowls to him. And he just steps back, to say the least, and he's caught! He's caught and that is the Ashes retained by England! Australia have been beaten by 103 runs, Border remains not out 123 and Australia are all out for 402. Jim Laker will shortly be awarding the man of the match and one suspects that it might be a certain gentleman whose name begins with B.

AUSTRALIA
SECOND INNINGS
402 all out

Third Test, Headingley, 16-21 July 1981
England won by 18 runs

AUSTRALIA

J. Dyson b Dilley	102	c Taylor b Willis	34
G. M. Wood lbw b Botham	34	c Taylor b Botham	10
T. M. Chappell c Taylor b Willey	27	c Taylor b Willis	8
*K. J. Hughes c & b Botham	89	c Botham b Willis	0
R. J. Bright b Dilley	7	b Willis	19
G. N. Yallop c Taylor b Botham	58	c Gatting b Willis	0
A. R. Border lbw b Botham	8	b Old	0
†R. W. Marsh b Botham	28	c Dilley b Willis	4
G. F. Lawson c Taylor b Botham	13	c Taylor b Willis	1
D. K. Lillee not out	3	c Gatting b Willis	17
T. M. Alderman not out	0	not out	0
Extras (b4, lb13, nb12, w3)	32	(lb3, nb14, w1)	18
Total (9 wkts dec)	**401**		**111**

ENGLAND

G. A. Gooch lbw b Alderman	2	c Alderman b Lillee	0
G. Boycott b Lawson	12	lbw b Alderman	46
*J. M. Brearley c Marsh b Alderman	10	c Alderman b Lillee	14
D. I. Gower c Marsh b Lawson	24	c Border b Alderman	9
M. W. Gatting lbw b Lillee	15	lbw b Alderman	1
P. Willey b Lawson	8	c Dyson b Lillee	33
I. T. Botham c Marsh b Lillee	50	not out	149
†R. W. Taylor c Marsh b Lillee	5	c Bright b Alderman	1
G. R. Dilley c & b Lillee	13	b Alderman	56
C. M. Old c Border b Alderman	0	b Lawson	29
R. G. D. Willis not out	1	c Border b Alderman	2
Extras (b6, lb11, nb11, w6)	34	(b5, lb3, nb5, w3)	16
Total	**174**		**356**

BOWLING

ENGLAND	O	M	R	W		O	M	R	W
Willis	30	8	72	0	–	15.1	3	43	8
Old	43	14	91	0	–	9	1	21	1
Dilley	27	4	78	2	–	2	0	11	0
Botham	39	11	95	6	–	7	3	14	1
Willey	13	2	31	1	–	3	1	4	0
Boycott	3	2	2	0	–	–	–	–	–
AUSTRALIA									
Lillee	18.5	7	49	4	–	25	6	94	3
Alderman	19	4	59	3	–	35.3	6	135	6
Lawson	13	3	32	3	–	23	4	96	1
Bright	–	–	–	–	–	4	0	15	0

AUSTRALIA fall of wickets
FIRST INNINGS: 1-55, 2-149, 3-196, 4-220, 5-332, 6-354, 7-357, 8-396, 9-401.
SECOND INNINGS: 1-13, 2-56, 3-58, 4-58, 5-65, 6-68, 7-74, 8-75, 9-110.
ENGLAND fall of wickets
FIRST INNINGS: 1-12, 2-40, 3-42, 4-84, 5-87, 6-112, 7-148, 8-166, 9-167.
SECOND INNINGS: 1-0, 2-18, 3-37, 4-41, 5-105, 6-133, 7-135, 8-252, 9-319.

First Test at Trent Bridge, June 18-21
Australia won by four wickets
England 185 (Gatting 52) and 125 (Lillee 5-46, Alderman 5-62); Australia 179 (Border 63) and 132-6.

Second Test at Lord's, July 2-7
Match drawn
England 311 (Willey 82, Gatting 59, Lawson 7-81) and 265-8 dec (Gower 89, Boycott 60); Australia 345 (Border 64) and 90-4 (Wood 62*)

Fourth Test at Edgbaston, July 30-August 2
England won by 29 runs
England 189 (Alderman 5-42) and 219 (Bright 6-68); Australia 258 and 121 (Botham 5-11).

Fifth Test at Old Trafford, August 13-17
England won by 103 runs
England 231 (Tavaré 69, Allott 52*) and 404 (Botham 118, Tavaré 78, Knott 59, Emburey 57, Alderman 5-109); Australia 130 (Kent 52) and 402 (Border 123*, Yallop 114).

Sixth Test at The Oval, August 27-31
Match drawn
Australia 352 (Border 106*, Wood 66, Kent 54, Botham 6-125) and 344-9 dec (Wellham 103, Border 84, Marsh 52); England 314 (Boycott 137, Gatting 53, Lillee 7-89) and 261-7 (Knott 70*, Gatting 56, Brearley 51).

ENGLAND IN AUSTRALIA 1982/3

Commentators **Henry Blofeld, Mike Denness, Tony Lewis, Alan McGilvray, Paul Sheahan and Fred Trueman**

Some strange things had happened to England on the way to Melbourne, Christmas '82. Mike Brearley's replacement Keith Fletcher had himself been replaced by Bob Willis after a depressing tour of India and, although he had presided over victories against India and Pakistan at home, the first three Tests of the Australian tour had produced a draw and two defeats. Even more alarming had been an incident at Perth which resulted in the severe disruption of Terry Alderman's career. Alderman's attempt to rugby-tackle an aggressive pitch invader caused the Australian pace bowler a dislocated shoulder, ending his participation in the series. England arrived in Melbourne needing to win the two remaining   to hold onto the Ashes and huge crowds descended on Boxing Day to witness the ritual slaughter of the Poms. All was going to plan when Greg Chappell put them in and the openers, Graeme Fowler and Geoff Cook, were sent back by Jeff Thomson and Rodney Hogg with only 25 runs on the board. Gower went straight after lunch and it was 56 for 3 but Chris Tavaré, whose defensive batting had made him Australians' 'man-you-love-to-hate', now came in, and with Allan Lamb, he rather uncharacteristically started to carry the game to the Australians, launching a particularly vigorous assault on the off spin of Bruce Yardley who eventually got his revenge with a gully catch off Thomson, but not before Tavaré had hit 15 fours in an innings of 89.

He and Lamb put on 161 for the fourth wicket. Only ten more runs came before Lamb skied a catch off Yardley to be out for 83 and he continued his revenge with three more wickets and England were polished off by Hogg. They were all out for 284.

Next day, Australia enjoyed a profitable first hour, before Willis brought on the fast bowler he had dropped for the Adelaide Test, Norman Cowans...

TONY LEWIS

Dyson 21 now. Cowans wipes the perspiration off his forehead with the left shirt sleeve, he's on his way again. Upright in the run up, strong – bowls and "How's that?" he says. He's out! lbw! His second Test wicket. A good straight ball by Cowans obviously got Dyson a little bit edgy through the extra speed and that was well bowled. Wicket to wicket a good action, but delivered from close to stumps, middle to middle and Dyson rather fell over, played across it. So Dyson, lbw 21. Australia are 55 for 1 ...

Chappell is at the crease, the drinks trolley has gone off. Cowans is doing some stretching exercises right back at the very beginning of his run. There are two men on the hook shot, as Cowans, upright in his run and quite strong in the shoulders and legs, comes in now – bowls ... Short. It's hooked ... It's in the air ... Lamb is under it. He catches it! And Chappell is out first ball! The England players crowd around Cowans, it was a marvellously judged catch by Lamb who had been put there specifically for the purpose. It was a good straight bouncer, Chappell hooked and Cowans is on a hat-trick.

Keppler Wessels, who had made his debut at Brisbane, saved the hat-trick and made 47 before Willis bowled him and, shortly after lunch, Botham did the same to Allan Border, who was having a wretched series. This time he went for 2 and Australia were 89 for 4. The afternoon, though, belonged to Kim Hughes and David Hookes who added 97. Pringle had Hookes caught behind on the stroke of tea for 53, but Rod Marsh carried on where he left off and, as the score mounted in the final session, England became resigned to a substantial Australian lead. Willis brought himself back for a final burst before the close and started a collapse by inducing Hughes to play on for 53, and it was 261 for 6. It was the start of a remarkable clatter of wickets in which the last five fell for only 26 runs.

Going in again at the start of the third day, England were only facing a deficit of three and, this time, Cook and Fowler enjoyed a more successful start, putting on 40 together before Thomson and Hogg removed Cook and

Keppler Wessels

his replacement, Tavaré. Then, Geoff Lawson had Gower caught behind for 3 and it was 45 for 3. Graeme Fowler had not always had the happiest of tours but now he dominated the afternoon session, making 65, before, typical of his luck, his toe was broken and he was bowled by Hogg. Lamb had shared a stand of 83 with him, but Hogg now added his scalp and it was 129 for 5. The match was right back in the Australians' grasp. Miller went at 160, but Derek Pringle came in to join Ian Botham and they started to pull the situation round...

PAUL SHEAHAN

If Australia is to maintain a chance of winning the game, and we've said time and time again that the Australians don't want to be chasing a total that's in excess of 220, then Botham is the man they must remove, and he is looking menacing. Thomson bowls and that, whipped away beautifully square of the wicket on the leg side, no fieldsmen in catching position there, and it rattles into the boundary. Four more to Botham – 46 now – and that brings up the England 200 for the loss of 6 wickets. That looks a good deal more comforting to the England players in the pavilion.

Well, that's forced a move from the gully for Hookes, out to a backward square leg position. Thomson again in ... short and he's caught! Botham is out caught by Chappell from the bowling of Thomson for 46 and England loses its 7th wicket with the score at 201.

Well, it seemed a pretty innocuous delivery, not a great deal of venom in it, but Botham again not moving his feet greatly, flung the bat at it and caught an outside edge and it flew very comfortably to Greg Chappell.

**ENGLAND
SECOND INNINGS
201-7**

Pringle now found support from Bob Taylor, who made 37 in an eighth wicket stand of 61. Pringle's excellent innings ended at 280 when he had made 42. It was not quite the end as Cowans gave a couple of strong heaves to the boundary in his ten and England were all out at the close of the third day for 294. Australia would have two days to make 292 to win and secure the Ashes.

On the fourth morning, for the first time in his three-Test career, Norman Cowans was entrusted with the new ball.

66It was Norman Cowans', (*left*) finest hour. It promised tremendous things, which never quite came. In that match, though, he showed great ability.**99** **Henry Blofeld**

ALAN McGILVRAY

Cowans goes in on his way now to bowl to the left hander Wessels — and bowls him! It came off the pad, I think. It whipped through defence and ran on to the stumps. It either came off the inside edge of the bat or the top of the pad but Wessels is out for 14, bowled by Cowans, and Australia lose their first wicket for 37.

That was a pretty slippery ball, that one. . .

TONY LEWIS

Cowans mops away the sweat, now turns again, the shirt clinging to his back as he works up the rhythm and bowls out to the off stump, he's caught! He's caught at cover! Caught by Gould who throws it many a mile in the sky! Off the back foot, a short ball that never quite came on. Chappell forcing, and caught very low at cover by Gould and Gould must think, at last, I've been able to contribute to this team effort in this tour, on this most important day of all.

Another wicket fell at 71, when Botham had Dyson caught at slip for 31, but, as the afternoon session wore on, the

AUSTRALIA
SECOND INNINGS
37-1

AUSTRALIA
SECOND INNINGS
39-2

balance began to shift inexorably in Australia's direction as Hughes and Hookes came together in another partnership, which added 100. It got no further. Miller had Hughes caught behind for 48. It was 171 for 4.

TONY LEWIS
Cowans coming in now, bowling to Hookes ... short, hooked away ... up in the air ... is Willis under it? He is! He's caught it! He's caught it! He's followed, like a Pied Piper, by his side, who all trail away from the pitch itself down to the boundary where Willis has ended up. That was a catch at mid-on running back and David Hookes walks off in entirely the opposite direction.

AUSTRALIA
SECOND INNINGS
173-5

David Hookes – another of Norman's conquests

HENRY BLOFELD
190 for 5, Australia needing another 102 more runs to win. Marsh is 13 not out, Border is 4. Cowans again to Marsh. What's going to happen now? Marsh is waiting for him. Cowans is there, bowls to Marsh and there's an appeal for lbw and he's out! He's lbw! Umpire Whitehead has his hand up and that did look a very obvious one. It hit him low down and I think it cannoned off the front pad onto the back one, plumb in line, middle and off, and there was no doubt about that. So Marsh is on his way, lbw bowled Cowans for 13 and Australia are now 190 for 6, Cowans has 4 for 44 and another huge sigh of relief for England...

AUSTRALIA
SECOND INNINGS
190-6

HENRY BLOFELD
Here's Cowans, in now, bowls to Yardley – short – and he's bowled him! He's bowled him! And that one

torpedoed. It just didn't get up an inch. It hit the middle and off stump about 4 inches up. There was no way in the world he could have played that. He got in the position to hook and he was dead. It really was a grub. . .

AUSTRALIA
SECOND INNINGS
190-7

TONY LEWIS
Pringle polishes, turns, tip-toes and now bowls . . . Hooked by Lawson . . . It's up in the air, Cowans is under it. Will he catch it? He does, he catches it! Cowans at fine leg, good bowling by Pringle because they knew that Lawson did not like the short stuff. He hooked it, it went high and who would have been under that? Well I'm glad it was Norman Cowans, because he took it so easily. A reverse palm catch and all the team go out to congratulate him. They slap all the hands in West Indian style and Lawson trails off. So Lawson caught Cowans bowled Pringle 7, 202 for 8. . .

AUSTRALIA
SECOND INNINGS
202-8

PAUL SHEAHAN
Eight for 218 and Australia really struggling now as Hogg faces the hero of this innings, Norman Cowans . . . and he's hit on the pads . . . and it's out! Yes, he's been given out, lbw. The ball struck the front pad of Hogg, but Hogg really only played 6 inches or so in front of the crease and was struck a very firm blow, low near the ankle and there is no doubt in my mind that the ball would have hit the stumps.

AUSTRALIA
SECOND INNINGS
218-9

It really was Cowans' day. With his sixth wicket of the match he had brought England to the brink of victory. Of the batsmen, only the out-of-form Allan Border remained, joined now by the number eleven, Jeff Thomson, with 74 more runs needed for victory. England's technique now was to offer Border singles in order to bowl at Thomson. It was an embarrassing failure which brought Australia another 38 runs before the close and played Border back into form. Australians were able to dream that night of an improbable victory – or rain.

Incredibly, on the final morning several thousand optimistic Australians did come to the MCG for a day which might only have lasted one ball. Listening on the radio at home the Test Match Special audience shared the tension of those in the commentary box as the wicket still did not fall and the big new electronic scoreboard registered Australia's steady progress.

66 I can remember saying on the radio towards the closing stages, "England have at least nine captains out there. Unfortunately Bob Willis is not one of them." We saw the continuation of this extraordinary ploy where they pushed the field back for Allan Border and gave him runs and then tried to attack Jeff Thomson, who's anything but a complete mug with the bat, as we saw in the World Cup Final of 1975. And he pushed and prodded and gradually the runs came on a wicket that wasn't playing that badly. It was a very nervewracking morning. Many of us lost our fingernails as what seemed to be a certain English victory turned into what seemed an absolutely certain Australian victory. **99**   **Henry Blofeld**

Miller (*above*) catches the rebound, England win by three runs and the disappointment of Thomson and Border (*below*) is evident.

Six runs were needed as Willis bowled to Border. Two runs came off the second ball of the over and then off the fifth ball of the over Border hit a hard shot which Geoff Cook fielded well at mid-wicket to prevent any run. Border remained at the non-striker's end for Botham's new over.

HENRY BLOFELD
Ian Botham is going to have one last crack at Jeff Thomson. 288 for 9, 4 to win for Australia, 3 to tie, Thomson has 21 and Border has 62. And Botham now bowls to Thomson. Thomson plays . . . He drops it . . . and he's out! He's caught in the slips! Tavaré knocked it up and it was Miller who caught the rebound. England have won by 3 runs and the England fielders are running off the ground, snatching the stumps. Cowans has got 2 of them and poor Thomson and Border walk back utterly dejected.

Well, that was Botham's hundredth wicket against Australia and what a magnificent moment! England have won this fourth Test Match by 3 runs, equalling the lowest margin of victory. Australia beat England by 3 runs at Manchester in 1902. What an astonishing end to the match. Thomson pushed at Botham, Tavaré knocked the ball up and he couldn't hold on but Miller, from first slip, came round behind him, took the catch and so Thomson was out. Caught by Miller, bowled by Botham for 21, Australia all out 288, Border not out 62 and England have won by 3 runs.

That remarkable win had kept England in the series, but a draw a few days later in Sydney ensured that Australia regained possession of the Ashes – for the next couple of years at least.

Fourth Test, Melbourne, 26-30 December 1982
England won by 3 runs

ENGLAND

G. Cook c Chappell b Thomson	10	c Yardley b Thomson	26
G. Fowler c Chappell b Hogg	4	b Hogg	65
C. J. Tavaré c Yardley b Thomson	89	b Hogg	0
D. I. Gower c Marsh b Hogg	18	c Marsh b Lawson	3
A. J. Lamb c Dyson b Yardley	83	c Marsh b Hogg	26
I. T. Botham c Wessels b Yardley	27	c Chappell b Thomson	46
G. Miller c Border b Yardley	10	lbw b Lawson	14
D. R. Pringle c Wessels b Hogg	9	c Marsh b Lawson	42
†R. W. Taylor c Marsh b Yardley	1	lbw b Thomson	37
*R. G. D. Willis not out	6	not out	8
N. G. Cowans c Lawson b Hogg	3	b Lawson	10
Extras (b3, lb6, w3, nb12)	24	(b2, lb9, nb6)	17
Total	**284**		**294**

AUSTRALIA

K. C. Wessels b Willis	47	b Cowans	14
J. Dyson lbw b Cowans	21	c Tavaré b Botham	31
*G. S. Chappell c Lamb b Cowans	0	c sub (Gould) b Cowans	2
K. J. Hughes b Willis	66	c Taylor b Miller	48
A. R. Border b Botham	2	not out	62
D. W. Hookes c Taylor b Pringle	53	c Willis b Cowans	68
†R. W. Marsh b Willis	53	lbw b Cowans	13
B. Yardley b Miller	9	b Cowans	0
G. F. Lawson c Fowler b Miller	0	c Cowans b Pringle	7
R. M. Hogg not out	8	lbw b Cowans	4
J. R. Thomson b Miller	1	c Miller b Botham	21
Extras (lb8, nb19)	27	(b5, lb9, w1, nb3)	18
Total	**287**		**288**

BOWLING

AUSTRALIA	O	M	R	W		O	M	R	W
Lawson	17	6	48	0	–	21.4	6	66	4
Hogg	23.3	6	69	4	–	22	5	64	3
Yardley	27	9	89	4	–	15	2	67	0
Thomson	13	2	49	2	–	21	3	74	3
Chappell	1	0	5	0	–	1	0	6	0
ENGLAND									
Willis	15	2	38	3	–	17	0	57	0
Botham	18	3	69	1	–	25.1	4	80	2
Cowans	16	0	69	2	–	26	6	77	6
Pringle	15	2	40	1	–	12	4	26	1
Miller	15	5	44	3	–	16	6	30	1

ENGLAND fall of wickets
FIRST INNINGS: 1-11, 2-25, 3-56, 4-217, 5-227, 6-259, 7-262, 8-268, 9-278.
SECOND INNINGS: 1-40, 2-41, 3-45, 4-128, 5-129, 6-160, 7-201, 8-262, 9-282.
AUSTRALIA fall of wickets
FIRST INNINGS: 1-55, 2-55, 3-83, 4-89, 5-180, 6-261, 7-276, 8-276, 9-278.
SECOND INNINGS: 1-37, 3-39, 3-71, 4-171, 5-173, 6-190, 7-190, 8-202, 9-218.

First Test at Perth, November 12-17
Match drawn
England 411 (Tavaré 89, Randall 78, Gower 72, Yardley 5-107) and 358 (Randall 115, Lamb 56, Lawson 5-108); Australia 424-9 dec (G. Chappell 117, Hughes 62, Hookes 56, Dyson 52, Lawson 50) and 73-2.

Second Test at Brisbane, November 26-December 1
Australia won by seven wickets
England 219 (Lamb 72, Lawson 6-47) and 309 (Fowler 83, Miller 60, Thomson 5-73, Lawson 5-87); Australia 341 (Wessels 162, G. Chappell 53, Yardley 53, Willis 5-66) and 190-3 (Hookes 66*)

Third Test at Adelaide, December 10-15
Australia won by eight wickets
Australia 438 (G. Chappell 115, Hughes 88) and 83-2; England 216 (Lamb 82, Gower 60) and 304 (Gower 114, Botham 58, Lawson 5-66).

Fifth Test at Sydney, January 2-7
Match drawn
Australia 314 (Border 89, Dyson 79) and 382 (Hughes 137, Border 83, Wessels 53); England 237 (Gower 70, Randall 70, Thomson 5-50) and 314-7 (Hemmings 95).

165

AUSTRALIA IN ENGLAND 1985

The Fifth Test, **Edgbaston,** *August 15-20*
Commentators **Brian Johnston, Alan McGilvray, Tony Lewis and Henry Blofeld**
Summarisers **Fred Trueman and Jack Bannister.**

Gower and Gatting

In 1985 a spirit of optimism pervaded English cricket. It had been born on the highly successful tour of India, in which England in unprecedented fashion had come back from losing the First Test to take the series. The golden boy, David Gower, was captain and, every bit as significant, his vice captain Mike Gatting had at last emerged as a Test batsman of true class. For the moment the previous summer's thrashing by the West Indies could be forgotten. Australia, meanwhile, had been playing the West Indies and, despite spinning them to defeat in Sydney, had lost the series 3-1.

At Headingley, in the First Test, England's victory was built on one of the new-found successes of their

Tim Robinson

winter tour, Tim Robinson. His 175 helped England to 533 and a five wicket win. But at Lord's it was the Australian captain, Allan Border, who made the big hundred – 196 – and Australia who demonstrated how the one success of their last summer had been achieved, as leg spinner Bob Holland took 5 wickets in the second innings to back up Craig McDermott's 6 in the first.

The Third and Fourth Tests were badly affected by rain and so the teams came to Birmingham all square with two to play. For the first two days it seemed that the weather would again prevent any result. Australia had been put in to bat and, after the delays, a dogged 83 from Keppler Wessels and an unbeaten half century by Geoff Lawson, they had reached 335 for 8 by the Friday evening. Richard Ellison had enjoyed a splendid day taking 5 wickets with his swing bowling, but surely Australia were, at the very least, safe from defeat when Saturday's play began …

Allan Border

ALAN McGILVRAY

And we're going to have an over I think, from Ellison.

It'll be Thomson in strike. He's on 28 and 53 to Lawson now. Umpire Shepherd calls Ellison in, and he's on his way. And, his first ball to Thomson, Thomson plays a good length ball out on the off side. He goes for a quick single. You'll be out, Lawson, if he hits . . . and he's out! I think he's out, yes he is! Thomson called for a run but Lawson was very slow to get going. He stopped and then Thomson kept going and Gower came in, underarmed the return, hit the stumps and Lawson was well short of his crease.

Well, what a great break for England. A run out off the first ball of the day but it was Thomson's call and Lawson failed to get going . . .

Something else is happening now. We've got another field change, Edmonds goes close in to backward point; well close enough at eighteen yards and Holland plays it in the air . . . and he's caught by Edmonds.

So, in the first over of the day, Australia have been dismissed for 335. A great performance for Ellison who has taken 6 wickets for 77.

AUSTRALIA
FIRST INNINGS
335-9

AUSTRALIA
FIRST INNINGS
335 all out

David Gower

ENGLAND
FIRST INNINGS
237-1

ENGLAND
FIRST INNINGS
253-1

So, a quarter of an hour into the third day, England started their first innings. With the score at 38, Graham Gooch gave Jeff Thomson his 200th Test wicket and his 100th against England. But the rest of the day belonged to England and, in particular, to the in-form Tim Robinson and David Gower . . .

TONY LEWIS
We welcome our World Service listeners wherever you are with the news that England have had a marvellous day and are batting now, 233 for 1. Robinson, who is facing, is 96 not out and David Gower 93 not out. So this has been a long partnership. In comes Thomson. Short . . . hooked away with tremendous power and flourish by Robinson and what a superb way to reach a century. He lay back and he applied the full face of the blade to it. I didn't see it off the bat. The next thing I saw was a small ball boy in a navy tracksuit picking the ball up at square leg. Off comes the helmet, up goes the bat, acknowledgement from Tim Robinson. He gets a century and now England are 237 for 1.

BRIAN JOHNSTON
Here is Thomson. Bowls it outside the off stump and Gower's gone for that one. It's four runs through extra cover. Four runs and Gower has gone up to 101 and England also 250 up, 253 for 1. So two centuries up on the board and one doesn't see that so often these days for England. It's a cheering sight for English eyes anyhow. 107 under Robinson, 101 under Gower, a lovely fluent stroke through extra cover and I'll give you the details of the innings in a second. Loud applause from the crowd, and the answer is that he had 169 balls, 247 minutes, he's hit 13 fours. Those are the details for him, so well done Mr. Gower, played very well, a captain's innings.

We'll give you the full details of this partnership in a moment but England have passed the Australian total in 80 overs.

Here is this one from Holland, and down the pitch goes Gower. He's found a gap on the leg side. It's going down to deep mid-wicket and it'll be fielded there, there is the 300 partnership, fielded by O'Donnell right out at deep wicket and these two have put on 300, Robinson and Gower, and the

crowd applauding. 338 for 1 and it's taken 306 minutes and the crowd really appreciating this. I'm really very pleased, I'm sorry for any Australian listeners. There can't be much joy listening but here is an English crowd revelling in the sunshine, which we haven't had much of, who have been given a treat today and I'm sorry if we sounded a bit too pleased.

By the close of that third day, England were 355 for 1 and their enterprising batting had given them an outside chance of victory.

On Monday morning, Robinson was bowled by Lawson for 148 with the score 463. His stand of 331 with Gower had been the second highest for England's second wicket against Australia. But Gower carried on, joined now by the ideal man to see him to a double century, Mike Gatting. Together they added another 94 before a tired Gower was caught at point off Lawson for 215, making the score 463 for 3.

ENGLAND FIRST INNINGS 338-1

66There are many people in Australia who, if they had to list the two or three players in the world they'd most like to watch, would almost invariably pick Gower amongst them. David Gower at his best is the most wonderful player. I suppose that on that tour Australia did not have really genuine pace bowling that counted and, when that happens, life becomes easier. Whenever you think of someone like Gower failing you have to turn to the West Indies. But left handers have that grace that doesn't seem to be given to right handers. **99**   **Henry Blofeld**

❝The thing about Gower is that people always say he is too laid back etc. But if you look at the figures – 7,000 runs in 100 Test matches – that's 70 per Test match which anyone would settle for.

We always pull his leg about being laid back and stuff but, of course, underneath it all he hides a deep feeling.

I don't think it should matter if, at times, he appears a little detached. It's aggravating at times, you think he's not caring and all that. But everyone does things in different ways. He didn't have a bad record as captain except he had the bad luck to play two series against the West Indies, and lost all ten Tests. He's had the ordeal by fire, as it were, and people forget also that he was quite a success in the West Indies in terms of his personal performances.**❞**

Brian Johnston

If Australia rejoiced to see the back of Gower, they now had Gatting and Allan Lamb to contend with and the runs continued to flow – 109 of them for the fourth wicket …

TONY LEWIS
Lamb is 46 now, and facing McDermott who tries again, runs away from us, past umpire Constant and bowls again on the leg side. It's in the air … and he's caught. Caught at mid-wicket! What a fine catch that was. Well, you'd have thought the ball was perfectly placed for four through the on-side but it was intercepted by Graeme Wood in the air, moving to his left very quickly and caught just above shoulder height with both hands. So Lamb retreats — caught Wood, bowled McDermott for 46 and England have lost their fourth wicket for 572.

JACK BANNISTER
A good innings, good partnership and now the person who everyone's been waiting for since the fall of Tim Robinson's wicket, Ian Botham.

TONY LEWIS

Well, it's a great super roar for, I suppose we must say, a superstar. It's well beyond the average welcome for any batsman in professional cricket because Ian Botham seems to have risen above the ordinary by his performance, by his attitude, by his appearance — that blonde highlighted hair, the multicoloured wrist band and the bat with the red rubber grip. And, of course, the daunting prospect for Australia is that at 572 for 4, in comes the premier hitter in the country.

Right, well another scene is set. A very defensive scene for Ian Botham who now takes guard and waits for McDermott. And they'd love to get Botham out, of course. He bowls, outside the off stump. That's 6. A colossal blow and Botham walks away to square leg. Well, it was a decent length ball and it just disappeared over long on and that's his 75th six of this season.

What a way to get off the mark! Now, an adjustment to the field. There is now a long off and a long on and McDermott comes in again to the outrageous Botham. Pitched well up ... he aims a vicious blow at that too, miscues and the ball runs to Wood at mid wicket. Now, what has David Gower told him? He's probably said 'I'm going to bat for 20 minutes, half an hour, give it a go'; and Botham inspects the carpentry at the bottom of this huge bat of his which might well have a crack, but he is prepared to prod the pitch as McDermott walks back very thoughtfully. Now, where is he about to bowl this? He'd love to bowl unplayable yorkers, ball after ball. The last one was a good one. In he comes and that's a tremendous blow again. That's 6. Straight 6, long on. Botham again walks away like some caged animal half way to square leg, now turns and comes back. Severely chastened, McDermott walks back like a naughty schoolboy, upright, almost marching, receives the ball back from a fielder. Down below us here, Hilditch is right on the line but two colossal 6's over long on, and you always pray that this can continue unless you're Australian or, I think, unless you're a realist because how long can it go on? McDermott bowls — tremendous slogging shot ... that's gone for 4 at square leg!

I must give you the score. It's 588 for 4. Botham has scored 16 off four balls. Meanwhile Gatting, almost unseen now, is 95 not out.

❝My great memory of that match is Botham striding out to face McDermott and hitting his first ball into that coconut-shy stand underneath the Press Box for 6. If ever a side could have been demoralised by one stroke it was Australia then.

The wheels fell off that Australian side towards the end of that tour as comprehensively as ever I've seen, since Australia lost in South Africa in '69/'70.❞

Henry Blofeld

Botham's innings was not greatly prolonged, indeed it lasted only seven balls in all before he was caught on the square leg boundary for 18 off a full toss from McDermott. The spotlight could return to Mike Gatting ...

**ENGLAND
FIRST INNINGS
595-5 dec**

TONY LEWIS
Border plays the game of nerves with Gatting and brings in Keppler Wessels from deep cover to orthodox cover saving one. Four in an arc in that cover area, saving the one, and three on the on side and McDermott ploughs in again past umpire Constant. Bowls ... tapped on the on side ... a misfield at mid-wicket and that's Gatting's century! And not only is it a century, a second in successive innings, it is also the England declaration. At 595 for 5, Mike Gatting acknowledges applause and strides off in his England cap, and stocky, smart walk. Raises the bat, 100 not out. So there is the declaration, England 595 for 5, a lead of 260.

In the latter stages of the fourth day, Australia were batting again in the face of that substantial, and all too rapidly acquired, English first innings lead. Botham removed Hilditch in what was becoming an almost ritual fashion, caught on the long leg boundary hooking recklessly, and Australia were in more trouble at 10 for 1. Wood and Wessels ground their way towards the close of play ...

TONY LEWIS
It's been a good crowd for a Monday. Plenty of seats available but still a very good turn out and the Rea Bank stand, the stand which skirts the tiny river Rea away to our right, has been full on every day and that seems to be the stand of vocal enthusiasm with maybe a little criticism from time to time. In comes Ellison ... a slower one ... He's caught! Wessels is caught behind the stumps by Downton, and how well that was bowled! It was slow, it was in the air, it was drifting across and Wessels went for once for a cover drive, followed through, it nicked the edge, Downton took it low and all the England players gather around Downton. Ellison polishes the ball and looks forward to the next one. A valuable wicket indeed. Thirty-two for 2 the Australian score, and Wessels takes off helmet and pads away back to the pavilion.

JACK BANNISTER *Nightwatchman time.*

Richard Ellison

TONY LEWIS

Thirty-two for 2. It's Bob Holland who's come in with 25 minutes to play out. That's rather a long time for a nightwatcher. There are always these great arguments in the dressing room with the nightwatchman saying 'I'm not available until a quarter to, skip, fifteen minutes is my maximum.' But so much at stake here. It's not just this match, not just this situation, but the Ashes themselves. Well Holland has taken guard. He's very keen to get on with it and so are the three slips, two gullies. As Ellison races in now from the City end and bowls … forward … strikes him on the pad! … Up go the arms! He's out, lbw, and Bob Holland, poor Bob Holland, the nightwatchman limps away. He played a stumbling shot across the stumps. It struck him just below the knee. David Constant had no hesitation in giving him out and so Richard Ellison is on a hat-trick and Australia stumble — 32 for 3. . .

BRIAN JOHNSTON

David Constant looks very strange, an umpire in an eye shade — Like in those American movies — the newspaper men always have them, with their sleeves rolled up with iron clips round them, and an eye shade and a cigar. He hasn't got a cigar and I'm not sure about his clips round his shirt sleeve. Anyhow, here's Ellison, rather tall and strong, bowls this one and it's up in the air and it's going to be caught at cover by Robinson, is it? He's there and he's caught it! So, Wood is caught Robinson, bowled Ellison. He is out for 10. Australia 35 for 4. Ellison has now taken nine wickets in the match. Australia in a wee bit of trouble. I don't know quite what Wood was trying to do, but it skied right up and Robinson took the catch . . . So, here's Ellison bowling to Border now. Edmonds very close in now on the leg side, and he's out! He's bowled, he's bowled! Border is bowled by Ellison and 36 for 5, Australia. Border bowled Ellison for 2. Ten wickets to Ellison in the match so far and the England team are cock-a-hoop and back comes Border, looking very dejected, as well he might. Thirty-six for 5, Fred, it's incredible.

FRED TRUEMAN

Well, this, of course, is the aftermath of the pasting the Australian bowlers have taken. They're down and at the moment they're getting very close to out.

Ellison sends back Holland

AUSTRALIA
SECOND INNINGS
32-3

AUSTRALIA
SECOND INNINGS
35-4

AUSTRALIA
SECOND INNINGS
36-5

66Ellison showed what good swing bowling can do. He bowled his outswingers and he bowled them well, swinging it late. Again it showed the brainwashing that genuine fast bowling has done. Here, instead of the fast, short ball, the batsmen were offered a new problem, which you would have thought they would have known how to cope with. It was the sort of success a new leg spinner is liable to have.99 **Henry Blofeld**

Ellison in command

Waking on the final morning with their score 37 for 5, the bruised and battered Australians must have been delighted to see steady drizzle in Birmingham. Would England's unpredictable weather deny them at the last?

A frustrating morning passed by under gloomy skies. And as the minutes ticked by, Ellison's glorious breakthrough the previous evening seemed more and more as if it was going to be a wasted effort. Lunch was taken with the destiny of the Ashes themselves in the hands of the weather gods. Eventually, in mid-afternoon, the battle was resumed. But, agonisingly for England, the delay had given Australia fresh hope.

Greg Ritchie and Wayne Phillips took up the fight with just over half the day to go and for a long time thwarted the England attack. It began to look as though they could save the match, as they posted Australia's hundred up and Phillips completed a fine half century ...

BRIAN JOHNSTON
Phillips certainly picks the right ball, and when he does, he hits it very hard. Back comes Edmonds, tossing the ball from hand to hand. Comes up now, bowls to Phillips, quicker one, short outside the off stump and there's an appeal. He hit it hard into the ground. Shepherd is now talking to Constant. Now what is this for? Off Lamb is that it?

JACK BANNISTER *He's given him out!*

BRIAN JOHNSTON
He's given him out! So Phillips, going for one off the back foot hit it hard and it went off ... what was it, Banners?

JACK BANNISTER
Some part of Lamb's leg and Gower caught the rebound. Clearly the only doubt was whether it had come straight back up, or whether it had yorked Lamb, so to speak, actually on the ankle.

BRIAN JOHNSTON *Well that's a blow for Australia, 113 for 6.*
JACK BANNISTER *It's a blow for Lamb as well.*

Allan Border argued later that there had been enough doubt about the decision for the umpires, (without the benefit of television replay, which clearly showed that they were right), not to have given the catch. Border claimed that wicket was to cost Australia the match.

❝I had not the slightest doubt that it was out. These freak things do seem to happen to a side that is out of luck. Phillips was just the sort of chap who might have saved that match for Australia, so it was a crucial blow.❞   **Henry Blofeld**

The controversial incident at Edgbaston: Wayne Phillips hits a ball from Phil Edmonds which strikes Allan Lamb ... the ball bounces up ... David Gower claims the catch ... Gower, Ian Botham and Edmonds wait for the umpire's decision, which is answered, after delay, in the affirmative.
Allan Border claimed there was too much doubt for the umpires to give Phillips out and that the decision probably cost Australia the match

Scenes of jubilation of the players' balcony at The Oval

AUSTRALIA
SECOND INNINGS
129 all out

Australia abruptly slid to 142 all out, defeated by an innings and 118 runs. England just needed not to lose at The Oval to regain the Ashes. There never seemed to be any doubt about the result, from the moment that Graham Gooch and David Gower put on 351 for England's second wicket. Gooch making 196 and Gower 157. Australia offered little resistance and the slide on the final morning was alarmingly rapid when Botham had taken his sixth wicket of the match and Ellison his seventh. For Test Match Special, it was a nostalgic morning as Alan McGilvray completed his last commentary ...

 ALAN McGILVRAY
Well, this has been a very decisive win that England are about to achieve. They've deserved it. The sides, when they came here, I thought, were pretty even. But England have steadily become a little better. They've become more solid — more purposeful. The better side has clearly won this series. We're watching Les Taylor go in now and Bennett hits it and he's caught and bowled! And that's the end of the match! All out, 129 and the margin was an innings and 94 runs. England have won the Ashes back and I wish them luck in the West Indies. If they continue in the form they're showing now, they'll give them a shake-up over there. Well, that's my story. I say congratulations to you England commentators and thanks for the support you've given me ...

 BRIAN JOHNSTON
A lovely scene here with the crowd coming across the ground waving at McGillers. And from all of us here in the box a very happy retirement.

On a balcony below, David Gower held high a replica of the Ashes his side had just won. It was a golden moment for English cricket, and the mood even encouraged some to believe the McGilvray prediction that England would 'give the West Indies a shake-up' during the coming winter. But, eight months later, there had been another five-nil 'blackwash' and Gower was on the point of losing the captaincy. Let's hope he savoured that Oval afternoon to the full.

Fifth Test, Edgbaston, 15-20 August 1985
England won by an innings and 118 runs

AUSTRALIA

G. M. Wood c Edmonds b Botham	19	c Robinson b Ellison	10
A.M.J. Hilditch c Downton b Edmonds	39	c Ellison b Botham	10
K. C. Wessels c Downton b Ellison	83	c Downton b Ellison	10
*A. R. Border c Edmonds b Ellison	45	b Ellison	2
G. M. Ritchie c Botham b Ellison	8	c Lamb b Emburey	20
†W. B. Phillips c Robinson b Ellison	15	c Gower b Edmonds	59
S. P. O'Donnell c Downton b Taylor	1	b Botham	11
G. F. Lawson run out (Gower)	53	c Gower b Edmonds	3
C.J. McDermott c Gower b Ellison	35	c Edmonds b Botham	8
J. R. Thomson not out	28	not out	4
R. G. Holland c Edmonds b Ellison	0	lbw b Ellison	0
Extras (lb4, w1, nb4)	9	(b1, lb3, nb1)	5
Total	**335**		**142**

ENGLAND

G. A. Gooch c Phillips b Thomson	19
R. T. Robinson b Lawson	148
*D. I. Gower c Border b Lawson	215
M. W. Gatting not out	100
A. J. Lamb c Wood b McDermott	46
I. T. Botham c Thomson b McDermott	18
†P. R. Downton not out	0
J. E. Emburey	
R. M. Ellison	did not bat
P. H. Edmonds	
L. B. Taylor	
Extras (b7, lb20, nb22)	49
Total (5 wickets declared)	**595**

BOWLING

ENGLAND	O	M	R	W		O	M	R	W
Botham	27	1	108	1	–	14.1	2	52	3
Taylor	26	5	78	1	–	13	4	27	0
Ellison	31.5	9	77	6	–	9	3	27	4
Edmonds	20	4	47	1	–	15	9	13	2
Emburey	9	2	21	0	–	13	5	19	1
AUSTRALIA									
Lawson	37	1	135	2					
McDermott	31	2	155	2					
Thomson	19	1	101	1					
Holland	25	4	95	0					
O'Donnell	16	3	69	0					
Border	6	1	13	0					

AUSTRALIA fall of wickets
FIRST INNINGS: 1-44, 2-92, 3-189, 4-191, 5-207, 6-208, 7-218, 8-276, 9-335.
SECOND INNINGS: 1-10, 2-32, 3-32, 4-35, 5-36, 6-113, 7-117, 8-120, 9-137.
ENGLAND fall of wickets
FIRST INNINGS: 1-38, 2-369, 3-463, 4-572, 5-592.

First Test at Headingley, June 13-18
England won by five wickets
Australia 331 (Hilditch 119) and 324 (Phillips 91, Hilditch 80, Wessels 64, Emburey 5-82); England 533 (Robinson 175, Botham 60, Downton 54, Gatting 53) and 123-5.

Second Test at Lord's, June 27-July 2
Australia won by four wickets
England 290 (Gower 86, McDermott 6-70) and 261 (Botham 85, Gatting 75*, Holland 5-68); Australia 425 (Border 196, Ritchie 94, Botham 5-109) and 127-6.

Third Test at Trent Bridge, July 11-16
Match drawn
England 456 (Gower 166, Gatting 74, Gooch 70, Lawson 5-103) and 196-2 (Robinson 77*); Australia 539 (Wood 172, Ritchie 146).

Fourth Test at Old Trafford, August 1-6
Match drawn
Australia 257 (Boon 61) and 340-5 (Border 146*, Wessels 50); England 482-9 dec (Gatting 160, Gooch 74, Lamb 67, McDermott 8-141).

Sixth Test at The Oval, August 29-September 3
England won by an innings and 94 runs
England 464 (Gooch 196, Gower 157); Australia 241 (Ritchie 64*) and 129 (Border 58, Ellison 5-46).

ENGLAND IN AUSTRALIA 1986-7

Commentators **Christopher Martin-Jenkins, Graham Dawson, Jim Maxwell and Neville Oliver**
Principal Summariser **Norman O'Neill**

KANGAROO

    These Pommies have got our Ashes

LION

    There'll be some spiffing clashes

KANGAROO

    We're hunting lion this summer, yes indeed.

    We've never had a sharper looking bunch

LION

    I fear we could be heading for a crunch

KANGAROO

    So bring the trophy with yer

    There's a lesson we're going to give yer

    This summer's gonna really pack a punch

CHORUS

    Come on Aussie, Come on . . .

The scriptwriters who prepare the marketing hype for Australia's Channel 9 Television in the sorry belief that a series for the Ashes needs such treatment were really having a field day. As Mike Gatting's team arrived from an English summer in which thay had lost to India and New Zealand, following a whitewash in the West Indies, they were jaded and unsuccessful. Australians had every reason to believe that their side, just returned with some honour from India, really could live up to the nightly television advertisement in which an irreverent, but lovably scruffy kangaroo faced a suitably pompous looking lion.

The early games against the states only served to underline the opinion of one of the English journalists covering the tour that Gatting's side "couldn't bat, couldn't bowl and couldn't field." Gatting suggested later that this was just the sort of provocation his team needed to fire them up as they headed from a disastrous draw in Perth against Western Australia to Brisbane for the First Test. But two important decisions had just been made in the management team. David Gower, the displaced captain who had lost the job after one Test of the previous summer, was drafted onto the selection committee and Gatting made the decision to bat at number three in the Test match.

When the First Test started, on November 14, all the received wisdom about Brisbane suggested that the side winning the toss would put the opposition in and would expect to do a lot of early damage to them. Australia, in any case had noticed England's susceptibility to left arm pace and Australia had two purveyors of this in Bruce Reid and Chris Matthews, who for this reason was preferred to Geoff Lawson.

So it was with a certain amount of dismay that England supporters learned that Allan Border had won the toss and invited England to bat. It was all following the ad-men's script. And even though the new ball was used with a somewhat wayward profiligacy, Australia did claim a wicket within the first hour with the score only 15, when Chris Broad was caught behind off Reid for 8. So Gatting's decision to go in at 3 was being tested early on. He rose to the occasion:

Mike Gatting

66That was a most significant decision. Originally the planning was that Gower would go in at 3 and Gatting at 5. But as it was, Mike went in at that first wicket, faced the music, was his usual positive self, played an absolutely splendid innings and really from the time that he started to get on top of the bowling, England were on top in that match.**99**
Christopher Martin-Jenkins

Only one other wicket fell on that first day of the series and that was Gatting himself, just after he had posted the century partnership with Bill Athey, bowled off his pads by Merv Hughes, the fastest of the Australian bowlers, for 61. To have shown such character on the first day in making 198 for 2 was a great psychological filip for

England, which was not shaken by the early loss the next day of the overnight batsmen – Lamb lbw to Hughes for 40 and Athey caught behind off Matthews for 76. The loss of Gower before he had scored, though, might have done . . .

CHRISTOPHER MARTIN-JENKINS
Hughes bowls to Gower, Gower is caught! dropped at first slip by Matthews. Well I said we would find out what sort of a catcher he was because Gower is almost inevitably going to do that early in his innings. A disappointed Hughes following through almost to Gower's eyeballs there. It was a bit short on the off stump, he went for that familiar Gower force off the back foot, and Matthews had a difficult chance high to his right, got both hands to it and spilt it.

66 That was a crucial moment in the series, because he was to be a key batsman throughout. He is such a brilliant player, with a particular liking for playing against Australia and a particularly good record against them, and undoubtedly Australians fear David Gower as well as admire him. He can be like the nursery rhyme, when he is good, he's very, very good and when he's bad he's horrid, so the fact that he was dropped before he had scored at a time when he really looked as though he had not a clue how to bat was most significant. He was at his worst. By his own admission he had lost all confidence, but now he grafted it out, and that is not a word you would normally associate with David Gower. 99
Christopher Martin-Jenkins

While Gower was making a shaky start, though, Ian Botham, playing on what would, the following Australian season, be his home ground, after his signing for Queensland, was playing as though it was already home. With Gower looking more and more solid, the pair added the second century partnership of the innings and it was 316 before Gower was out for 51. Jack Richards' debut as England's wicket keeper was started with a duck and Emburey also went cheaply, but 351 for 7 was not the end as another new cap, Philip DeFreitas, started playing extravagant shots inspired by the example of his mentor, Ian Botham, who had already reached his century...

JIM MAXWELL

Matthews to him, he is down and he swings at this, look at this guys, straight over the sight screen 6, bang. It landed over the dog track, right over the sight screen, over long off, the third 6 of Botham's innings, he is 132. The entertainment rolls on, 7 for 424, they have added 73. There have been some crashing shots — a 6 behind point, one behind square, a pull, and that straight almost off driven blow and here he is down again, he is having a lash at it and it is going for 6 again I think, it is a big hit, where will that one land? Over the top, near the dog track and into the Sir Gordon Chalk building for 6 more. How do you bowl to a man in that mood? Two 6's in the over. He is 138 and he is playing with complete disdain. Waugh trying to get the break, bowls to DeFreitas, he swings at this and it goes over Matthews' head and it goes to the boundary in front of square for 4 more. What a start to your Test career, opening up with Botham here in this partnership. He is playing a free hand now, anything near the pads he is wheeling in to and he has made 29. Now, he watches Waugh and hits this away on the on side, another well-timed shot, chipping it away through mid-wicket, 4 more, that was magnificently timed by DeFreitas and he whistles along to 33 and takes the score to 438.

ENGLAND
FIRST INNINGS
430-7

ENGLAND
FIRST INNINGS
438-7

Steve Waugh, a young Australian all-rounder just starting to make his mark at this level, captured both wickets, but not before they had added 92 for the eighth wicket. Botham made 138 and DeFreitas 40. DeFreitas' day was not finished, either. On that second evening he took the new ball with Graham Dilley...

181

AUSTRALIA
FIRST INNINGS
27-1

66It was an explosive start, but after that Phillip DeFreitas *(right)* did not make such an impact on the tour until the last few weeks of it in the World Series Cup one-day games, when, because of his freshness, youth, enthusiasm and his tremendous innate ability he came through again to be probably the best bowler at that stage. With a lot of ambition and ability, he promised to be a tremendous asset to England for many years.99
Christopher Martin-Jenkins

JIM MAXWELL
DeFreitas, bowls again, a short ball and he is caught!
Caught by Broad at mid-wicket. It was short, well worked out by DeFreitas because previously Boon had played that shot when there was no one at mid-wicket. He dropped one short and Boon — really it was a thimble and pea job there, a short ball, he did not get hold of it and he hit it straight down the throat of Broad at mid-wicket. Boon is out, DeFreitas takes his first wicket in Test cricket and Australia 1 for 27.

The next day, though, was Dilley's. He took five wickets as Australia struggled to avoid the follow-on. Early on it was the opener, Geoff Marsh, who could find no permanent support before Dilley had him caught behind for 56. But Australia passed 200 with 6 wickets down and the follow-on only 57 runs away. Now it was the eccentric off spinner, Greg Matthews, who had to watch the wickets tumble at the other end as he was left 56 not out in Australia's 248 – nine short of saving the follow-on. On the eve of a rest day, Gatting had no hesitation about inviting the Australians to bat again.

The fourth day was a hard one in humid, hot conditions with Australia trying to grind their way out of trouble and England to chip away. At the centre of the recovery act again was Geoff Marsh, who batted through the day, reaching a century by the end of it. At the other end, Botham, Emburey and Dilley each got some reward, but a fourth wicket stand of 113 between Marsh and Greg

Ritchie took Australia to the brink of a lead, which they had taken by the close with five wickets down.

For the first half hour of the final day England suffered the agonies of striving for the all-important breakthrough until Gatting was on the point of introducing spin, when DeFreitas ended the heroic performance of Marsh by cutting one back to bowl him for 110. The remaining four wickets could only manage 20 runs and England's target was 75. They did manage to lose three wickets en route, but the victory was all the sweeter for the pre-publicity and the eight defeats in the previous 11 Tests since they had last played Australia – and won.

The Australian press looked for a scapegoat and chose Allan Border. England, meanwhile, returned to their pre-Test form with an embarrassing defeat at the hands of New South Wales in Newcastle.

In the Second Test at Perth, England really seemed to miss the chance to go two up in the series. After winning the toss they made a daunting 592 for 8 declared, based on an opening stand of 223 by Chris Broad, who made 162, and Bill Athey, with 96. The left-handed Broad, who had left Gloucestershire for Nottinghamshire to win an England cap, and Athey who had gone to Gloucestershire from Yorkshire to escape the internal strife, had appeared to be something of a makeshift opening pair. They were to give the lie to that . . .

❝If you have a settled opening partnership, consistently putting on stands of 50 plus and often over 100, you are a long way towards winning any Test series and Chris Broad's *(above)* performance in this series was quite remarkable. Bill Athey *(left)* played exactly as had been hoped; a tough, dependable, correct player. Mickey Stewart, the cricket manager, had drummed it into both of them that they needed to take plenty of time in Test cricket. They did not not need to play anything wide of the stumps in the first half hour. They should see the new ball off and suddenly it would seem easier.**❞**

Christopher Martin-Jenkins

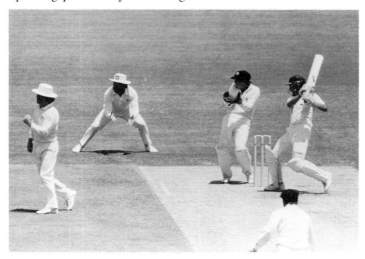

Their splendid start was followed by hundreds from Gower and, in his second Test, Jack Richards, who has been a slightly controversial choice as wicketkeeper for the First Test ahead of Bruce French.

In reply to that massive total, Australia this time managed to save the follow-on, by just nine runs, thanks to 125 from Border and 71 from Waugh. On the fourth day, England were now in need of quick runs for a declaration before the close. But though Gower made a sparkling 48 and Gatting 70, England were held in check by Australia and Gatting was just nervous enough about losing to delay that declaration till the morning. The cracks in the pitch on which England had pinned their hopes refused to help the bowlers and Australia saved the game easily. Indeed during the day the frustration caused Ian Botham to put too much into an attempted bouncer and strain a rib muscle which was to rule him out of the Third Test in Adelaide.

Before that Adelaide Test, Mike Gatting found himself in the midst of a controversy he could well have done without. On the first morning of the match against Victoria, the captain himself overslept and David Gower had to toss up on his behalf. At Adelaide, therefore, Gatting had some ground to make up. He did it in fine style by making 100 in England's reply to Australia's 514 for 5 declared. David Boon, who must have been on the verge of losing his place, had made 103, Dean Jones 93 and there had been scores in the seventies from Border, Greg Matthews and Waugh, as Australia pressed on to the declaration to underline yet again what a useful player he was becoming. But Chris Broad and Bill Athey put together another hundred partnership for the first wicket and Broad went on when Athey was bowled by the leg spinner, Peter Sleep, for 55.

He made his second century of the series so that despite four wickets apiece for Reid and Sleep, England finished only 59 runs behind. Australia had needed to enforce a follow-on and now had really run out of time, but Border did use the second innings to make his 21st Test century.

So England were able to enjoy Christmas in Melbourne with the knowledge that just a draw in one of the remaining two Tests would retain the Ashes for them. However, for the Test starting on Boxing Day, Botham, though fit to bat was not likely to be able to bowl flat out and Graham Dilley, England's most threatening strike bowler, was unfit.

Small took the new ball with DeFreitas when Gatting had won the toss and put Australia in. He did not have to wait long to make his mark …

CHRISTOPHER MARTIN-JENKINS

It strikes me that England in this test find themselves in a similar position to Australia in the first because they have two very inexperienced opening bowlers, Small, looking a bit nervous at the moment, runs in, bowls and he is caught at second slip, Boon went forward and Botham is back in the act very early on because it was he who took the catch at tummy height, a nice comfortable slip catch and Boon out, shaking his head now as he walks towards the pavilion in an almost identical way as he was out to Graham Dilley in the second innings of the Perth Test match. He pushed forward down the line of off stump, the ball left him a little and Boon edged it at comfortable catching height to Botham and Australia have lost their first wicket with the score 16.

Ian Botham had been immediately in the action with that

66This really would have been the tour on which Graham Dilley came of age if only he could have gone through it without an injury, but he did bowl marvellously — a formidable opening bowler and Dilley firing on all cylinders in even three Tests out of five would be worth having. It was touch and go whether Small *(left)* or Neil Foster replaced him and in the end the selectors chose Small because he could be relied upon to put the ball in the right place, on the off stump on a good length, and he thoroughly justified his selection.**99**

Christopher Martin-Jenkins

**AUSTRALIA
FIRST INNINGS
16-1**

185

catch and after trying Emburey to see what the off spinner might do, Gatting called up Botham to bowl . . .

GRAHAM DAWSON
Six men on the off side to Botham, he bowls, short, Marsh, oh he is caught behind by Richards, a beautiful catch, a bouncing delivery from Botham, Marsh went for the hook stroke it was fast – a top edge, Richards went up and he dragged it down from above his head with both gloves, a beautiful catch by Richards and as Ray Bright was saying, you cannot keep Botham out, he has a wicket in his first over, Marsh caught Richards, bowled Botham, 17, Jones is 17 and Australia 2 for 44. . .

JIM MAXWELL
Botham bowls again, it is short and it is cut and it is almost caught, . . . it is caught by Richards. Botham dropping short again, Border going to cut, a bottom edge and a good catch low down by Richards. For a moment I was not certain that it had carried to him, but it had all right and that is an excellent break for England, Botham, picks up Allan Border, his second wicket of the morning.

At 108 there was another slip catch by Botham off Small, this time to dismiss Waugh for 10 and, after that, the collapse was catastrophic. By tea on the first day Botham and Small – 5 wickets each – had bowled Australia out for just 141. By the close England were even more firmly in the driving seat at 95 for 1 having lost only Athey for 21.

Australia had to wait until after lunch on the second day to capture another wicket and by then England were 22 runs in the lead. Gatting was out for 40, hooking at Reid but soon after that Chris Broad wrote his name in the history books and ensured his position as Australia's "International Cricketer of the Year" with his third century in successive Tests. He made 112 before he was caught behind off Hughes. Lamb made 43, but England must have been a bit disappointed with the score of 349, which might have been even lower but for the whirling bat of Gladstone Small who made 21 not out going in last in a 10th wicket stand of 30.

Australia started their second innings at the start of the third day, 208 behind. Mike Gatting admits to feeling

AUSTRALIA
FIRST INNINGS
44-2

AUSTRALIA
FIRST INNINGS
80-3

Small dismisses Reid during his five-wicket performance

at the time that they had already been let off the hook, and that they would probably get a lead of about 150. Only two wickets fell before lunch, with England now looking to the spinners to wear the rest away gradually.

By tea Australia were only 39 runs behind, but 5 wickets down. The abruptness of the finish was a considerable shock, and just 40 minutes after tea …

CHRISTOPHER MARTIN-JENKINS
In comes Edmonds and bowls, gives it a lot of air –
Bowls him! Well bowled Edmonds, that was a good bit of bowling indeed. He held it back, Waugh went down to drive for the run that would have got his 50 but the ball turned just enough, beat him half in the air and half on the turn as he drove over the top of it and bowled him. Waugh is out and with him goes Australia's last slim hope of keeping England in the field even in to the fourth day of this match. It now looks as though they are doomed. It is 185 for 8 and a deserved second wicket for Philippe Edmonds…

CHRISTOPHER MARTIN-JENKINS
There are two men out, three men out in fact for the big hit, square leg, deep mid-wicket and long on. It looks as though Australia are going to go down with two big fast bowlers blazing their guns as … Emburey bowls him! Forward went McDermott, the ball went on with the arm and knocked off the middle and off bail. Botham goes to collect the ball which had run down to third man, McDermott walks out disconsolately, 9 wickets down now for 189 and England are on the verge of retaining the Ashes – just one wicket to go…

CHRISTOPHER MARTIN-JENKINS
In comes Edmonds and he swings it, it is a good sweep but he is going to be caught! And England have won the Ashes, caught by Gladstone Small and what an appropriate ending because Small, I think, will probably be named man of the match and what a moment for the man who came in only as a reserve for England at the last moment, to take the catch which retains the Ashes for England and wins the Fourth Test match to give England an unassailable 2-nil lead in this 1986/87 series.

Small was indeed the man of the match, and England had won by an innings and 14 runs with over an hour and two

AUSTRALIA
FIRST INNINGS
185-8

AUSTRALIA
SECOND INNINGS
189-9

AUSTRALIA
SECOND INNINGS
194 all out

Gladstone Small – man of the match

Chris Broad – International
Cricketer of the Year, 1986

whole days to spare. Mike Gatting called it his greatest moment since he had won his first Test cap.

Before the Fifth Test, England were in Perth, where they won a four nation one-day tournament which was part of the America's Cup festivities. It was clear that once again the script had been misread when England and Pakistan, rather than Australia and the West Indies, contested the final.

The Sydney Test, on the anticipated turning pitch, was preceded by a major Australian selectorial surprise which led to the off spinner, Peter Taylor, earning the title "Peter Who?". There were many who were convinced that the selectors had sent for the wrong man, intending a batsman, Mark Taylor, as Peter could not be sure of his place in his state side. But he played and was to be the man of the match.

First, though, came Dean Jones, who came in at 3 and 184 not out when the innings ended at 343. England recovered from a frightful start to make 275 and then John Emburey enjoyed one of his finest hours with seven wickets in the Australian second innings of 251 which was due in no small part to Peter Taylor's 42. It was turning out to be a classic Test match. Now, though, England needed 320, a stern target in the last innings of a Test on a turning pitch. The captain's own innings of 96 was at the heart of a brave chase, which would have been abandoned to the needs of safety much earlier if the Ashes were not already secure. In the end it went to the penultimate over with England hanging on grimly, but going down by 55 runs.

Australia now abandoned itself to another extravanganza of one day cricket, the World Series Cup, which England again carried off. But they and all but the most susceptible onlookers knew that the Ashes remained the supreme prize in cricket.

Fourth Test, Melbourne, 26-28 December 1986
England won by an innings and 14 runs

AUSTRALIA

G. R. Marsh c Richards b Botham	17	run out		60
D. C. Boon c Botham b Small	7	c Gatting b Small		8
D. M. Jones c Gower b Small	59	c Gatting b DeFreitas		21
*A. R. Border c Richards b Botham	15	c Emburey b Small		34
S. R. Waugh c Botham b Small	10	b Edmonds		49
G. R. J. Matthews c Botham b Small	14	b Emburey		0
P. R. Sleep c Richards b Small	0	run out		6
†T. J. Zoehrer b Botham	5	c Athey b Edmonds		1
C. J. McDermott c Richards b Botham	0	b Emburey		1
M. G. Hughes c Richards b Botham	2	c Small b Edmonds		8
B. A. Reid not out	2	not out		0
Extras (b1, lb1, w1, nb7)	10	(lb3, w1, nb2)		6
Total	**141**			**194**

ENGLAND

B. C. Broad c Zoehrer b Hughes	112
C. W. J. Athey lbw b Reid	21
*M. W. Gatting c Hughes b Reid	40
A. J. Lamb c Zoehrer b Reid	43
D. I. Gower c Matthews b Sleep	7
I. T. Botham c Zoehrer b McDermott	29
†C. J. Richards c Marsh b Reid	3
P. A. J. DeFreitas c Matthews b McDermott	7
J. E. Emburey c & b McDermott	22
P. H. Edmonds lbw b McDermott	19
G. C. Small not out	21
Extras (b6, lb7, w1, nb11)	25
Total	**349**

BOWLING

ENGLAND	O	M	R	W		O	M	R	W
Small	22.4	7	48	5	–	15	3	40	2
DeFreitas	11	1	30	0	–	12	1	44	1
Emburey	4	1	16	0	–	20	5	43	2
Botham	16	4	41	5	–	7	1	19	0
Gatting	1	0	4	0	–	–	–	–	–
Edmonds	–	–	–	–	–	19.4	5	45	3

AUSTRALIA	O	M	R	W
McDermott	26.5	4	83	4
Hughes	30	3	94	1
Reid	28	5	78	4
Waugh	8	4	16	0
Sleep	28	4	65	1

AUSTRALIA fall of wickets
FIRST INNINGS: 1-16, 2-44, 3-80, 4-108, 5-118, 6-118, 7-129, 8-133, 9-137.
SECOND INNINGS: 1-13, 2-48, 3-113, 4-153, 5-153, 6-175, 7-180, 8-185, 9-189.
ENGLAND fall of wickets
FIRST INNINGS: 1-58, 2-163, 3-198, 4-219, 5-251, 6-273, 7-277, 8-289, 9-319.

First Test at Brisbane, November 14-19
England won by seven wickets
England 456 (Botham 138, Athey 76, Gatting 61, Gower 51) and 77-3; Australia 248 (Matthews 56*, Marsh 56, Dilley 5-68) and 282 (Marsh 110, Emburey 5-80).

Second Test at Perth, November 28-December 3
Match drawn
England 592-8 dec (Broad 162, Gower 136, Richards 133, Athey 96) and 199-8 dec (Gatting 70, Waugh 5-69); Australia 401 (Border 125, Waugh 71) and 197-4 (Jones 69).

Third Test at Adelaide, December 12-16
Match drawn
Australia 514-5 dec (Boon 103, Jones 93, Waugh 79*, Matthews 73*, Border 70) and 201-3 dec (Border 100*); England 455 (Broad 116, Gatting 100, Athey 55) and 39-2.

Fifth Test at Sydney, January 10-15
Australia won by 55 runs
Australia 343 (Jones 184*, Small 5-75) and 251 (Waugh 73, Emburey 7-78); England 275 (Gower 72, Emburey 69, Taylor 6-78) and 264 (Gatting 96, Sleep 5-72).

189

INDEX

Note: Names of commentators generally are given in **bold** type. Interviews are shown by page numbers in **bold** type. Page numbers in *italic* type indicate photographs.